Surviving in the City

The Urban Informal Sector in Latin America

J. J. THOMAS

Pluto Press

LONDON • EAST HAVEN, CT

First published 1995 by Pluto Press
345 Archway Road, London N6 5AA
and 140 Commerce Street, East Haven, CT 06512, USA

99 98 97 96 95   5 4 3 2 1

British Library Cataloguing in Publication Data
A catalogue record for this book is available from the British Library

ISBN 0 7453 0827 9 hb

Library of Congress Cataloging in Publication Data
Thomas, J.J. 1933–
Surviving in the city : the urban informal sector in Latin America
/ J.J. Thomas.
         p.   cm.—(Critical studies on Latin America)
     Includes bibliographical references and index.
     ISBN 0–7453–0827–9 hbk
     1. Informal sector (Economics)—Latin America.
     2. Urbanization—Latin America. I. Title. II. Series.
     HD2346.L38T48 1995
     330—dc20

Designed typeset and produced for Pluto Press by
Chase Production Services, Chipping Norton, OX7 5QR
Printed in the EC by T J Press, Padstow, England

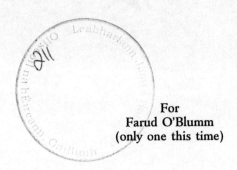

For
Farud O'Blumm
(only one this time)

Contents

LIST OF BOXES

LIST OF TABLES

Series Foreword

The *Critical Studies on Latin America* series introduces the reader to the major debates amongst scholars attempting to theorize political, social and economic developments in Latin America as it approaches the millenium.

Economically, the region has been engaged for some years in major structural changes, opening itself up to highly competitive international markets while tackling the tasks of growth and development in a rapidly changing economic environment. The agency of this development passed in the course of the 1980s from the interventionist state of the postwar decades, to the historically weak private sector, with uneven outcomes in different countries. However, the debate between 'state' and 'market' is by no means over in the region. The urgency of investment in the educational and infrastructural requisites for sustained growth point to a continued role for the state, while a strong state is seen by some as the only means to protect the disadvantaged from the logic of market forces. This logic is transforming labour markets, the relationship between formal and informal economics, the nature of the agrarian sector and the balance between rural and urban development. Persistent tension between growth and equity, wealth creation and poverty alleviation reflect the continued polarization within Latin American societies. Economic transformation and social upheaval reach to the heart of existing class, gender and ethnic relations, creating diverse arenas of challenge and change in these relations. One such arena is politics, where realignments and redefinitions are underway throughout the region. Social movements have challenged the very boundaries of what has hitherto been perceived as 'politics' and the actors associated with it. The role of political parties and political leaders in the relationship between state and society is being reconstructed, albeit in different ways, in many parts of Latin America. Some hail the emergence of a dynamic 'civil society' in the region, while others are more cautious in their analysis of the shifting relationship between the state and its citizens, and between authoritarian and democratic political formations. Latin America, described in the 1960s as a 'living museum' for the way its old order has always survived the process of modernization, has entered a new epoch of flux and transition.

This series does not intend to predict outcome nor provide detailed studies of all aspects of change, but to outline debates and contested approaches in significant areas. The aim is to enrich our understanding of Latin America at one of the region's most dynamic periods of development and to foster discussion on the different ways to conceptualize the processes taking place.

Jenny Pearce, Series Editor
Department of Peace Studies
University of Bradford
January 1995

Preface

This book is the second in a series of texts, edited by Jenny Pearce, who writes in her General Preface that 'The series introduces the reader to the major debates amongst scholars attempting to theorise political, social and economic development in Latin America as it approaches the millenium'. Given this overall objective, the aim of this text is to examine the impact of economic change in Latin America on urban labour markets in recent decades and to discuss the question of how the poor survive in the cities.

Given the debt crisis and periods of structural adjustment, most Latin American countries experienced falling (or at best very slow rates of growth of) employment in the modern (formal) sector during the 1970s and 1980s; in the absence of social security or unemployment benefits, those without work could not afford to be unemployed. The solution for many in this position was to create their own employment in a variety of activities that have been grouped together under the umbrella concept of the urban informal sector, the phenomenon that is examined in this book.

There have been a number of debates concerning the urban informal sector. For example, are the operations of the urban informal sector independent of the formal sector, or are the sectors linked? If the second possibility is correct, is the urban informal sector exploited by the formal sector, or is the relationship beneficial to the urban informal sector? Is the urban informal sector best characterised as a set of incipient capitalists held in check by regulations and bureaucracy (as Hernando de Soto suggests) or does the sector have more to do with poverty and survival in the city? To what extent did early studies of the urban informal sector, which ignored questions of gender, produce a distorted picture of the sector? These and other issues will be explored below.

The author writes as an econometrician with an interest in urban problems and poverty in Latin America. From this perspective, it is important to measure and quantify the phenomena to be studied, since without such information it is difficult to gauge the magnitude of the problems being discussed or evaluate the range of policy options that are available and their likely costs and benefits. To speculate on the future of the urban poor it is necessary to have numerical data, even if the numbers only approximate the reality being investigated.

However, while there is an emphasis on economic and statistical factors, it is not exclusive. Other social scientists have made important contributions to the analysis of the issues discussed in this book and the reader will be directed to their work where it is relevant to the discussion through the extensive bibliography that is provided at the end of the text.

Latin Americans love acronyms and these have been used extensively in the text. They are defined as they are introduced and, as a reminder to the reader, a listing of acronyms and their definitions is given in the *List of Acronyms* that follows this *Preface*.

The original idea for this book came from Jenny Pearce's invitation for me to write a text for her series and I am grateful to her for an opportunity to reflect on the issues discussed here at greater length than is possible in research papers or journal articles. I also appreciated her good humour and encouragement during the writing of the text, when I was aiming at, but not always hitting, publishing deadlines.

As usual, I owe a particular debt to my partner, Luba Mumford, who read early drafts of all the chapters and greatly reduced verbosity. Later versions of the complete text were read by Victor Bulmer-Thomas, Jenny Pearce and Eriko Togo, while Sylvia Chant and Peter Lloyd-Sherlock commented on some of the chapters and provided references in areas where they have considerable comparative advantage. Any merits in the text must be attributed to my following many of the helpful suggestions of those cited above, but failure to follow all their suggestions means that I take full responsibility for all errors of commission or omission and for the conclusions reached in the book.

J.J. Thomas
*London School of Economics
and Political Science*
28 March 1995

List of Acronymns

EAP: Economically Active Population – all men, women (and children) within age range eligible to work. The definition varies from country to country and is defined more specifically in the text.

EU: The European Union, formerly the European Economic Community (EEC).

FONCODES: *Fondo Nacional de Compensación y Desarrollo Social*, Peruvian governmental organisation set up to co-ordinate anti-poverty programmes in Peru.

GDI: Gross Domestic Investment – total domestic investment that has not been adjusted to allow for depreciation of the capital stock. (Gross Domestic Investment – Depreciation = Net Domestic Investment.)

GDP: Gross Domestic Product – measure of the national income of a country that is produced within the country in a given period, usually one year.

GNP: Gross National Product – measure of the national income of a country available for distribution in the country. Basically, GNP = GDP + net property income from abroad.

HDI: Human Development Index – a unweighted index based on life expectancy, education and income distribution – published in the United Nations Development Programme's (UNDP) annual *Human Development Report*.

IDESI: *Instituto de Desarrollo del Sector Informal* (Institute for the Development of the Informal Sector), an organisation providing credit for workers in the UIS in Peru.

IDB: Inter-American Development Bank, international organisation based in Washington DC.

IEA: Informal Economic Activity – economic activities that for various reasons are not included in the National Income Accounts (see Thomas (1992a)).

ILD: *Instituto Libertad y Democracia* (Institute of Liberty and Democracy), founded by Hernando de Soto in Lima.

ILO: International Labour Organisation – an organisation representing the tripartite interests of governments, employers and labour in countries that are affiliated to its conventions. It has been based at the International Labour Office in Geneva since it was founded by the League of Nations in 1919.

IMF: International Monetary Fund.

IMR: Infant Mortality Rate – see Table 4.2 for a definition.

INEGI: *Instituto Nacional de Estatística Geografía e Informática*, Mexico's National Statistical Institute.

ISI: Import Substituting Industrialisation – a policy adopted in many developing countries after World War II in which a programme of modernisation was carried out that aimed at developing domestic industrial output sufficiently to substitute for imported industrial goods from the developed countries.

LEB: Life Expectancy at Birth – see Table 4.2 for a definition.

OECD: Organisation for Economic Cooperation and Development. Founded in 1960, to replace OEEC (Organisation for European Economic Cooperation), which was founded in 1948.

NGO: Non-Governmental Organisation.

PCP: Petty Commodity Production – see Section 2.2.

PEM: *Programa de Empleo de Emergencia*, emergency employment programme operated in Chile under the Pinochet regime.

PREALC: *Programa Regional del Empleo para América Latina y el Caribe*, the ILO's regional office for Latin America and the Caribbean in its World Employment Programme (WEP), based in Santiago (Chile) from 1969 to 31 December 1993.

SAP: Structural Adjustment Programme – economic programme designed to cut government spending deficits, control the money supply, remove subsidies and restrictions on trade in order to change the structure of the economy towards a more market oriented system. Often imposed by the World Bank (WB) or International Monetary Fund (IMF) as the condition for providing further loans.

SENA: The National Apprenticeship Service in Colombia, responsible for providing training programmes and apprenticeships.

TED: Total External Debt – the sum of public, publicly guaranteed, and private non-guaranteed long-term debt, use of IMF credit and short-term debt.

TFR: Total Fertility Rate – see Table 4.2 for a definition.

UFS: Urban Formal Sector – defined in Chapter 2.

UIS: Urban Informal Sector – defined in Chapter 2.

UNDP: United Nations Development Programme.

UNICEF: United Nations Children's Fund.

WB: The International Bank for Reconstruction and Development (IBRD), better known as the World Bank.

WEP: World Employment Programme, a programme to encourage employment run by the ILO since the 1960s.

1 Surviving in the City

1.1 *Introduction*

One of the most striking locational changes since the end of World War II has been the massive urbanisation that has occurred in developing countries. As Hellman (1986, p. 216) noted:

> In the space of one generation, two hundred million people have moved from the countryside to the cities of Asia, Africa and Latin America, while the number of Third World cities of one million or more has grown from sixteen in 1950 to well over sixty today.

The data presented in Table 1.1 show that the urban percentage of the population has increased throughout the developing world, but that many of the countries in Latin America have reached much higher levels than in Africa or Asia; levels that are comparable with those found in the UK or the USA. High urban growth rates have continued throughout the period from 1965 to 1992 and in many Latin American countries a large percentage of the urban population lives in the major city.

Changes in the urban labour force were even more dramatic, as is illustrated in Table 1.2. The size of the urban Economically Active Population (EAP), as a percentage of the Total EAP, increased in all 17 countries and the average for Latin America rose from 43.5 per cent in 1950 to 64 per cent in 1980. The contrast between the smallest and largest also decreased markedly – in 1950 the smallest percentage was Honduras with 18.9 per cent and the largest was Uruguay with 77.8 per cent, whereas by 1980 the range was from 42.8 per cent in Honduras to 84.4 per cent in Argentina. While in 1950 only four countries had more than 50 per cent of the Total EAP in the urban environment and 11 were less than 40 per cent, by 1980 nine were over 60 per cent and none were less than 40 per cent.

In general, the reason for migrating to the cities was economic,

Table 1.1 *Urbanisation in Latin America (1965–91)*

Country	1			2		3		
	1965	1985	1991	1965 –80	1980 –91	1960	1980	1990
Argentina	76	84	87	2.2	1.8	46	45	41
Bolivia	40	44	52	2.9	4.0	47	44	34
Brazil	50	73	76	4.5	3.3	14	15	—3
Chile	72	83	86	2.6	2.2	38	38	36
Colombia	54	67	71	2.8	2.9	17	26	21
Ecuador	37	52	57	5.1	4.4	31	29	21
Paraguay	36	41	48	3.2	4.4	44	44	48
Peru	52	68	71	4.1	4.0	38	39	41
Uruguay	81	85	86	0.7	0.8	56	52	45
Venezuela	72	85	85	4.5	2.7	26	26	25
Costa Rica	38	45	48	3.7	3.7	67	64	72
El Salvador	39	43	45	3.5	3.1	31	29	26
Guatemala	34	41	40	3.6	3.5	41	36	23
Honduras	26	39	45	5.5	5.4	31	33	35
Nicaragua	43	56	60	4.6	3.9	41	47	46
Panama	36	41	54	3.4	2.9	61	66	37
Dominican Republic	35	56	61	5.3	3.9	50	54	52
Mexico	55	69	73	4.5	2.9	28	32	34
Africa[1]	19	32	36	5.8	5.4	30	38	33
Asia[2]	17	23	30	4.4	5.0	19	26	25
UK	87	92	89	0.5	0.2	24	20	14
USA	72	74	75	1.2	1.1	13	12	—3

Source: World Development Report 1988, Table 32, pp. 284–5 and *World Development Report 1993*, Table 31, pp. 298–9.

Key:
1 Urban population as a percentage of total population.
2 Average annual growth rate of urban population.
3 Percentage of urban population living in largest city.

Notes:
1 Unweighted average of 10 countries: Cameroon, Ghana, Kenya, Morocco, Nigeria, Senegal, Tanzania, Tunisia, Uganda and Zaire.
2 Unweighted average of 8 countries: Bangladesh, Burma, China, India, Nepal, Pakistan, the Philippines and Thailand.
3 In the *World Development Report 1993*, the information presented changed from 'Percentage of urban population in largest city' to 'Percentage of urban population in capital city'.

Table 1.2 *Urban Economically Active Population as Percentage of Total Economically Active Population (1950–80)*

Country	Year			
	1950	1960	1970	1980
Argentina	72.0	77.6	81.6	84.4
Bolivia	24.1	28.8	35.0	41.1
Brazil	39.2	47.2	53.5	62.1
Chile	62.9	65.0	69.8	74.2
Colombia	39.2	45.1	56.4	64.9
Ecuador	33.2	37.5	40.9	48.1
Paraguay	—	—	—	—
Peru	36.0	41.6	50.5	58.8
Uruguay	77.8	79.2	81.0	82.3
Venezuela	51.1	63.1	71.3	79.0
Costa Rica	42.0	47.8	57.0	65.3
El Salvador	32.2	36.7	42.0	47.5
Guatemala	31.4	36.2	39.8	44.5
Honduras	18.9	28.4	35.6	42.8
Nicaragua	30.3	37.2	47.5	57.8
Panama	46.7	49.7	59.6	66.2
Mexico	34.5	45.7	52.1	61.5
Dominican Republic	28.2	33.2	45.6	58.6
Latin America	43.5	50.5	56.7	64.0

Source: PREALC (1982), various tables.

with the rural poor seeking better job opportunities and better access to health and education than were available in the countryside, although this was not the case for all migrants in countries such as Colombia or Peru, where many sought to avoid the dangers of civil war or guerrilla activities by escaping to the safer anonymity of the city. In Central America, flight to relative safety often involved immigration – see Basok (1993) for an account of the survival of Salvadorean refugees in Costa Rica, and Morrison and May (1994) on Guatemala. This massive population move-

Table 1.3 *Economic Experiences of Latin American Countries (1970–91)*

Country	GDP		GDI		Inflation		TED	
	1970 –80	1980 –91	1970 –80	1980 –91	1970 –80	1980 –91	1980	1991
Argentina	2.9	–0.4	3.1	–6.9	133.9	416.9	27157	63707
Bolivia	4.5	0.3	2.3	–8.0	21.0	263.4	2700	4075
Brazil	8.1	2.5	8.9	–0.1	38.6	327.6	71046	116514
Chile	1.4	3.6	1.0	5.1	188.1	20.5	12081	17902
Colombia	5.4	3.7	5.0	–0.2	22.3	25.0	6941	17369
Ecuador	9.6	2.1	11.0	–2.4	13.8	38.0	5997	12469
Paraguay	8.5	2.7	18.6	0.3	12.7	25.1	954	2177
Peru	3.5	–0.4	6.5	–3.4	30.1	287.3	9386	20709
Uruguay	3.0	0.6	–	–5.9	65.1	64.4	1660	4189
Venezuela	3.5	1.5	7.1	–3.9	14.0	21.2	29345	34372
Costa Rica	5.7	3.1	9.2	4.4	15.3	22.9	2744	4043
El Salvador	4.2	1.0	7.3	2.3	10.7	17.4	911	2172
Guatemala	5.8	1.1	7.9	–0.7	10.5	15.9	1166	2704
Honduras	5.8	2.7	9.1	3.4	8.1	6.8	1470	3177
Nicaragua	1.1	–1.9	–	–5.3	12.8	583.7	2176	10446
Panama	4.4	0.5	0.3	–7.5	14.5	10.1	2974	6791
Mexico	6.3	1.2	8.3	–1.9	38.6	327.6	57378	101737

Source: All data from *World Development Report 1993* (World Bank, 1993a).

Key:
GDP: Average annual growth rate of GDP (%), Table 2, pp. 240–1.
GDI: Average annual growth rate of GDI (%), Table 8, pp. 252–3.
Inflation: Average annual rate of inflation (%), Table 1, pp. 238–9.
TED: (in US$ millions, converted at official exchange rates), Table 21, pp. 278–9.

ment was not planned by the governments of the countries concerned and, in general, they neither attempted to control it nor
dealt with its effects on the cities to which the migrants came.
What happened to the poor in the cities will be one of the themes
explored in this book, but before that can be done it is necessary
to examine the macroeconomic context within which the urbanisation took place.

1.2 *Modernisation, the Debt Crisis and Structural Adjustment*

Looking back over recent decades, some observers of Latin America may feel a certain nostalgia for the period before 1980. These were years of reasonable optimism, when the dominant economic policy was one of Import Substituting Industrialisation (ISI). The objective of the ISI policy was to reduce the dependency of developing countries on the export of primary products (such as copper from Chile, tin from Bolivia and bananas from the Caribbean) in return for the import of manufactured goods from the developed countries. The aim was to replace imported manufactured goods with locally produced goods and this was to be carried out by the modern private sector (often protected and subsidised by the state) and through the operation of state-run enterprises. A number of economic indicators seemed to suggest that the ISI policies were working, with the majority of the countries in the region experiencing growth in their Gross Domestic Production (GDP) and Gross Domestic Investment (GDI) (see Table 1.3).

The picture was not entirely rosy, however, since a number of countries in the region had experienced very high average annual rates of inflation and the Total External Debt (TED) also reached relatively high levels in most of the countries. These were indications that the growth in the years before 1980 had been obtained at a cost that might lead to problems in the future.

It was also true that in all the countries high proportions of the population still lived in conditions of extreme poverty and, as the data in Table 1.4 demonstrate, the distribution of income is extremely unequal in Latin America. On average, the bottom 20 per cent of the population receive less than 5 per cent of total income, while the top 20 per cent of the population receive 50 per cent or more.[1]

Brazil has the most extreme range of inequality and the Brazilian social commentator, Herbert de Souza, noted that: 'Brazil is really three nations in one: a rich country with a population the

---

1. The World Bank has published fewer data on income distribution for countries in Africa and Asia than for Latin America. For those countries where data are published, income distributions are unequal, but less so than in Latin America. For example, in both Africa and Asia the top 20 per cent of the population tend to have between 40 per cent and 50 per cent of the income. At the other end of the scale, in Asia the lowest quintile received nearly 10 per cent of total income, while in Africa the average was closer to Latin America.

Table 1.4 *Distribution of Income in Latin America (1970–91)*

Country	Year	Quintile				
		1	2	3	4	5
Argentina	1970	4.4	9.7	14.1	21.5	50.3
Bolivia	1990–91	5.6	9.7	14.5	22.0	48.2
Brazil	1972	2.0	5.0	9.4	17.0	66.6
	1989	2.1	4.9	8.9	16.8	67.5
Chile	1989	3.7	6.8	10.3	16.2	62.9
Colombia	1988	4.0	8.7	13.5	20.8	53.0
	1991	3.6	7.6	12.6	20.4	55.8
Ecuador	—	—	—	—	—	—
Paraguay	—	—	—	—	—	—
Peru	1972	1.9	5.1	11.0	21.0	61.0
	1985–86	4.9	9.2	13.7	21.0	51.4
Uruguay	—	—	—	—	—	—
Venezuela	1970	3.0	7.3	12.9	22.8	54.0
	1989	4.8	9.5	14.4	21.9	49.5
Costa Rica	1971	3.3	8.7	13.3	19.9	54.8
	1989	4.0	9.1	14.3	21.9	50.8
El Salvador	1976–77	5.5	10.0	14.8	22.4	47.3
Guatemala	1980	5.5	8.6	12.2	18.7	55.0
	1989	2.1	5.8	10.5	18.6	63.0
Honduras	1989	2.7	6.0	10.2	17.6	63.5
Nicaragua	—	—	—	—	—	—
Panama	1970	2.0	5.2	11.0	20.0	61.8
	1989	2.0	6.3	11.6	20.3	59.8
Dominican Republic	1989	4.2	7.9	12.5	19.7	55.6
Mexico	1977	2.9	7.0	12.0	20.4	57.7
	1984	4.1	7.8	12.3	19.9	55.9
Sweden	1981	8.0	13.2	17.4	24.5	36.9
UK	1979	5.8	11.5	18.2	25.0	39.5
	1988	4.6	10.0	16.8	24.3	44.3
USA	1980	5.3	11.9	17.9	25.0	39.9
	1985	4.7	11.0	17.4	25.0	41.9

Sources: World Development Report 1986, pp. 226–7, Table 24; 1990, pp. 236–7, Table 30; 1993, pp. 296–7, Table 30; 1994, pp. 220–1, Table 30.

Key:
Year = year in which income data collected.
1, 2, 3, 4, 5 = Percentage of income received by first (poorest), second, third, fourth and fifth (richest) quintiles of the population.

size of Canada's, a poor country with a population equal to Mexico's and a country of indigents as big as Argentina.' (REUTERS e-mail report from Washington DC, 11 December 1994).

It was argued that the solution to the problem of poverty was not a redistribution of income, but a successful ISI policy that would produce enough income growth in the economy for the fruits of modernisation to 'trickle down' to the poor. During this period, many governments were not concerned with the high rates of rural–urban migration, as it was assumed that the expansion of the modern sector would be sufficient to absorb the growing non-agricultural EAP. However, the difficulties of expanding employment in the public sector and the private industrialised sector fast enough to absorb the increases in the EAP were becoming clear and some commentators were investigating what was happening to those unable to find modern sector jobs.

The 1980s was not a kind decade to Latin America; the world recession, coupled with the debt crisis, caused severe problems for most of the countries in the region. As Table 1.3 shows, the average annual rates of growth of GDP and GDI fell for the majority of countries and were negative for a number of them. Price levels rose sharply in most of the countries, with six of them experiencing average rates of inflation of over 250 per cent per annum. High interest rates in the 1980s increased the debt burden and led to repayment problems, with the value of TED rising sharply for most of the countries in the region (see Table 1.3).

These problems and the need to reschedule the repayment of the external debt led many Latin American countries to undertake structural adjustment programmes (SAPs), often under pressure from the World Bank (WB) or the IMF.[2] These involved carrying out a variety of economic 'reforms' that were intended to free markets from restrictions, to reduce the size of state intervention in the economy and to increase competition, both domestically and internationally.

The popular perception is that the costs of adjustment were not shared equally among the population and that the poor paid a disproportionally high price for the economic changes that happened during this period. This proposition is not easy to evaluate, as there is conflicting evidence from various sources. For example,

---

2. For a discussion of structural adjustment programmes and the question of whether they cause poverty to increase, see Thomas (1993a) and the references given there. For further readings, see García (1993), Horton, Kanbur and Mazumdar (1994a, b), Khan (1993), Plant (1994), Sachs (1989), Turnham (1993) and World Bank (1993c).

UNDP (1993, p. 103, Table 1.3) presents data on the Human Development Index (HDI) – an unweighted index based on life expectancy, education and income distribution – for all the Latin American countries, showing that, with the exception of Nicaragua and Peru, the other countries showed improvements between 1970 and 1990. However, four more of the countries (Bolivia, El Salvador, Guatemala, Hondurus) had still only attained relatively low levels by 1990 and had HDI values of less than 0.600 (as compared with 0.964 for the UK, 0.976 for the USA and 0.983 for the highest ranking country, Japan).

However, even where the share of the national cake going to the poor increased, it was either part of an overall smaller cake or a cake that was growing more slowly than in the previous decade. In addition, the poor had to cope with the higher rates of inflation that occurred in most Latin American countries during the 1980s. There is evidence (see Gil Díaz, 1987 and World Bank, 1989b) that, as compared with the rich, the poor hold proportionally more of what little savings they have in the form of cash in local currency. They are therefore forced to pay the 'inflation tax' in full when the authorities finance a government deficit by printing money (see Cardoso and Helwege (1992, Chapter 6) for a full discussion of the effects of inflation). The rich have advantages over the poor, as they are able to save in the form of real assets, such as property, that retain their value in the face of inflation. Additionally, they are able to hold US dollars or shift their funds abroad to earn interest in countries that have more stable price levels.

The overall picture is difficult to capture completely in terms of international comparisons and we shall return to the question of poverty in Chapter 3, when we consider the data on individual countries.

The labour market was one of the many markets that was affected by changes brought about through structural adjustment programmes. As early as the 1970s, when the rate of increase in the non-agricultural EAP was greater than the rate of expansion of jobs through ISI policies, observers noted that while there was a rise in the rate of open unemployment (where open employment is defined as persons who are without work, but are seeking work and are available for work), it did not rise sufficiently to account for those members of the EAP who were not absorbed into the process of industrialisation. Since the poor could not afford to be unemployed in countries that did not provide social security payments or unemployment benefits, what had happened to them? When the evidence was collected, it became clear that they survived by creating their own employment. This is often very visible,

Box 1.1 Surviving on the Streets of Lima in the late 1980s

The major cities in Latin America differ in their locations and characters, but all have one thing in common – the high degree of activity in the streets. For example, the Peruvian capital Lima, which for many months of the year is covered in a sea mist produced by the cold waters of the Humboldt Current, is a city which has continued to grow rapidly from its 1981 population of 4.6 million inhabitants. In the centre of Lima are two important squares, the Plaza San Martin, with its grand hotels, cinemas, exclusive clubs and magazine stands, and the Plaza das Armas, which is flanked by the Cathedral, the Archbishop's Palace, the City Hall and the Presidential Palace. Connecting these two squares is the Jirón Unión, a pedestrianised street some five blocks long that is one of the main commercial streets in central Lima. On either side are shopping arcades and shops selling clothes, jewellery, food, records, books and souvenirs. Filling the street between the shops is a jostling crowd of street sellers offering a wide range of products. At the intersection of Unión with the Plaza San Martin and the Jirón Ocoña are groups of young men and women who, bundles of Intis and pocket calculators in hand, are prepared to change US dollars at black market rates. They are ignored by the policemen and policewomen who stand around in small groups on that side of the square, the latter in 'smart bottle-green suits with incongruous slits up the skirts' wearing long black boots and small revolvers in neat white holsters, carrying handbags and heavily made up, looking 'as though they were cast for a sado-masochist film, in which the violence is done to men by women'. (Daniels, 1986, p. 7.) Here also are gathered food sellers with small carts of the kind used by ice-cream sellers in Britain. However, given the climate of Lima, for most of the year they are offering not ice-cream but hot food, such as corn grilled on the cob, empanadas, or tamales wrapped in green banana leaves.

On Unión, the variety of goods for sale is wide; there are sellers of chocolate; sweets and cigarettes are on offer, either in packets or, more usually, individually; many goods are spread out on the ground – here cheap shoes in neat rows on plastic sheets and there shoelaces, ball-point pens, cheap trinkets or tubes of toothpaste, soaps, perfumes, mirrors, combs and shampoos, all lovingly arranged in elaborate mounds; cheap clothing is either spread out on the ground or carried on coathangers at arm's length by the sellers – shirts, many of which have been made by homeworkers and supplied to the sellers either directly by the makers or through wholesalers, and sweaters that are acrylic and machine-made, since the beautiful hand-knitted, alpaca sweaters are too expensive for this market and are to be found in the artisan shops for tourists on Belén, to the south of the Plaza. Other people are selling 'one-off' items, with two men here holding up a small coffee table and there two others with some bookshelves, while further on another man offers one elaborate electric chandelier.   *Continued*

The majority of the sellers are mestizo or Indian and the age range is wide, since in addition to the adults there are many children. Those older than about eleven or twelve generally operate independently or in small groups, particularly if they are boys. The girls and the smaller children normally work with their mother or older siblings and the smallest are often used as a kind of bait on the principle that it is hard to refuse to buy a sweet or some other small item if it is offered by a toddler.

More mobile are the shoe-shine boys, as well as the pickpockets who are said by the guidebooks to frequent this area and have earned the centre of Lima a dire warning in *The South American Handbook*.

Halfway along Unión is the elaborately carved facade of the church of La Merced and most of the beggars in the area seem to be concentrated around the doors of the church, where they are likely to catch the tourists both relatively stationary and in a mood to give alms to the poor.

The street is crowded with people, colour and noise. In addition to the hubbub of conversation between the sellers and the potential customers strolling by, there are the calls of the sellers, such as those selling lottery tickets with particularly 'lucky' numbers to offer, while the music shops add their contribution, mixing Western pop with Latin American music ancient and modern – Andean folk music and salsa. In a sheltered corner an old, small, blind, crippled Indian man is huddled against a wall strumming a small guitar, while the small girl who will lead him home at the end of his working day stands quietly beside him holding his crutches and a small tin in which to collect small coins from passers-by. Spaced along the street are public call boxes and here there are people selling the metal tokens needed for the telephone, shaking plastic bags of the tokens rhythmically, like maracas, to attract attention.

as is illustrated by the description in Box 1.1 of a street scene in Lima observed by the author in the late 1980s.

The main purpose of this text is to examine this missing group, whose members are neither working in the modern sector nor formally unemployed. How many of them are there? Who are they? What do they do? What are their socio-economic characteristics? Do they represent a homogeneous or a heterogeneous group?

Should governments encourage or discourage them and the activities in which they engage? How well do they survive? These are some of the questions we shall try to answer in the chapters that follow.

The concept of the Urban Informal Sector (UIS) was developed to analyse this missing group, but it has been the subject of much popular misunderstanding and the next section will categorise other forms of informal economic activities to put the UIS in a broader context and show what it is not, in preparation for discussing what it is.

1.3 *'Informality' and the Urban Informal Sector*

Since its 'invention' in the early 1970s, the concept of the UIS has attracted much interest, discussion and disagreement. Some have seen the UIS as a negative feature of developing countries, the survival of traditional (primitive) activities and methods of production that would (and should) disappear in the process of increased industrialisation and modernisation. Others have seen the UIS as containing a pool of potential entrepreneurial talent that should be encouraged to develop and become formalised. A third view is that the UIS is part of the international post-colonial capitalist system that has been allowed to survive because it supplies cheap goods to the urban proletariat and thus helps to keep down the cost of labour to the capitalist system.

These views and disagreements are among some of the issues to be discussed in this book. However, the reader should be warned from the outset that the study of the UIS is not easy, not least because there is no concensus over its definition. Lubell (1991, p. 19) quotes Professor Hans Singer of the Institute of Development Studies at the University of Sussex as saying 'An informal sector enterprise is like a giraffe; it's hard to describe but you know one when you see one'.

The question of precisely how to define and measure the size of the UIS will be left until the next chapter and here the discussion will put the UIS into a broader context of 'informality' and discuss what the UIS is *not*.

The author's experience has been that when, in answer to questions about his area of research, he confesses to having an interest in the working of the UIS, the reponse is a slight look of puzzlement on the part of the questioner that is usually followed by one of two further questions. Either 'Oh, you mean tax evasion and all that?' or 'Oh, that's all about drugs in Latin America, isn't it?' My answer to these questions is negative, since the UIS is the 'quasi-legal' part of a wider group of activities that include tax evasion and dealing in drugs, which I have referred to elsewhere (Thomas, 1992a) as Informal Economic Activity (IEA). IEA is defined to include activities of an economic nature that, for various reasons, are not fully reported in the National Income

Table 1.5 *The Structure of Informal Economic Activity*

Sector	Market transaction	Output	Production/ distribution
Household	No	Legal	Legal
Urban/Informal	Yes	Legal	'Quasi-Legal'
Irregular	Yes	Legal	Illegal
Criminal	Yes	Illegal	Illegal

Source: Based on Thomas (1992a, p. 6, Table 1.1).

Accounts. In order to concentrate on different dimensions of these activities it proved useful to classify them into four sectors, as shown in Table 1.5.

The advantage of this categorisation is that it avoids lumping a wide range of activities under one heading, which would have confused the issue and reduced the analytical power of the analysis, which has serious implications for the rational discussion of policy questions.

The *Household Sector* includes the value of housework and the goods and services generated in subsistence production. It differs from the other three sectors in the important sense that no market transactions are involved, since these goods and services are not sold, but are produced, distributed and consumed within the household or on the peasant's small plot of land as the case may be. Subsistence production is an important means of survival for the poor and, in rural locations, may represent most of the household's production and consumption. In the urban context, possibilities for subsistence production may be more limited, as it may be difficult to keep animals or grow crops in a Latin American city. However, these activities will still be important, as often women will make clothes for the family and both men and women will help build the house. We have little information on what value should be imputed to these non-market activities, but they represent an important part of the survival strategy for the urban poor.

The *Irregular Sector*, more popularly known as the Black (Underground, Subterranean or Shadow) Economy, produces legal goods and services, but breaks the law either in the production of the product (for example, through infringements of laws regarding industrial safety or the non-payment of minimum wages and other workers' contributions for pensions or social security) or in the distribution of the product (for example, through tax evasion) or both.

The irregular sector has been of great concern to the governments of many developed countries, since those who break these laws or evade tax are perceived as being well able to meet the costs of obeying the law and paying their taxes. As a result, great efforts have gone into the process of catching and prosecuting offenders. Given the criminal nature of these activities, it is difficult to obtain reliable data on how large this sector is, but estimates range from 5 per cent to 35 per cent of GNP for the United States and the United Kingdom. The author would argue for estimates towards the lower end of the scale (see Thomas, 1992a, Chapter 7).

Undoubtably tax evasion exists in developing countries, though governments seem very tolerant of the rich who evade their tax reponsibilities in comparison with the situation in many developed countries. In many Latin American countries, the direct taxes collected on income or property are a relatively small proportion of government revenue and governments rely on a battery of indirect taxes and special levies that often encourage smuggling and other forms of tax evasion (see Thomas, 1992a, Chapter 10).

The *Criminal Sector* differs from all the other sectors in that while it is involved in market transactions, the goods and services produced (drugs, robbery, prostitution – in some countries, extortion etc.) are illegal and therefore the production and distribution of these goods and services is also illegal. In the Latin American context, a major criminal activity is growing the raw materials for the production of banned drugs, as this region is the world's supplier of cocaine and has recently been making a significant contribution to the production of heroin.

While the considerable profits to be made from criminal activities by the professional drugdealer (*narcotraficante*) are generally out of the reach of those working in the UIS, some criminal activities may be in the range of opportunities they need to consider. For example, some may resort to robbery as a way of making money, while prostitution for both sexes, but especially for women and children, represents an alternative source of income.

While crime may be a survival strategy for some, it is not the dominant mode of operation of the poor in Latin America. The evidence from many surveys shows they are basically trying to make an honest income if they can. It is important to distinguish between legal and criminal activities, since the policy implications are different. For example, governments may seek to encourage legal informal activities, while discouraging those that are criminal.

13

The *Urban Informal Sector* is involved in market transactions, its output consisting of legal goods and services, while the production and/or distribution is 'quasi-legal'. What is the distinction between the 'quasi-legality' of the UIS and the illegality of the Irregular Sector? The answer is not entirely satisfactory for a general definition, as it rests on the attitude of the authorities and the degree of law enforcement. For example, the Irregular Sector is the subject of much interest on the part of politicians and the media in developed countries, such as the USA and the countries in the European Community, where the authorities devote considerable resources to attempts to catch tax evaders and punish them for their illegal activities. In contrast, many street traders in the cities of developing countries operate without licences – not to evade taxes, since their earnings are unlikely to be large enough to attract the tax collector, but because the authorities do not *formally* encourage such trading. However, in many cities street traders are tolerated by the authorities, at least for most of the time. They may be driven off the streets by the police as part of a temporary smartening up of the environment during important international events. This happened in Santo Domingo for the fifth centenary celebrations of Columbus' first voyage to the New World. However, once the dignitaries had departed, the traders returned to the streets and the police returned to buying sweets, food, cigarettes and other items from the street traders.

Essentially, the distinction being made is between *de jure* and *de facto* legality. In the Irregular Sector, those who break the law hide their activities, since they know the authorities are trying to enforce the law and will punish those they catch breaking it. In the UIS those flouting the rules and regulations are often very visible, but the reaction of the authorities may be either to ignore the law-breaking or to enforce the law only sporadically and incompletely.[3]

Why are these distinctions between the sectors important? The answer is that the different characteristics of the sectors lead to different reactions and policies on the part of governments and other authorities. Thus, housework and those types of subsistence production in the Household Sector that lie outside the market system tend to be ignored by the authorities while, at the other extreme, the illegal nature of the goods and services produced by

---

3. While this link between illegality and informality is important for discriminating between the UIS and the Irregular Sector and plays a key role in Hernando de Soto's view of 'informality', the next chapter will argue that it is only one element in the definition of the UIS.

the Criminal Sector attracts much attention from politicians, who may devote considerable resources to decreasing the activities of those involved in this sector.

The goods and services produced in both the UIS and the Irregular Sector are legal, so the authorities generally have no objection to the output, but may be concerned about the process of production and/or distribution. In the case of the Irregular Sector, if individuals are evading their tax liabilities, the authorities may encourage them to continue in their productive activities providing they pay their taxes. In the UIS, where the problem may not be tax evasion, but rather the inability of those working in the sector to satisfy the rules and regulations, the policy question may concern what needs to be done to enable the poor to improve their earning capacity through training or access to credit or changes in the rules and regulations. Given these differences in the policy analysis, it is important to see that the UIS is neither primarily about tax evasion nor about drugs in Latin America.

Part of the confusion over what constitutes the UIS arises from the fact that individuals may be involved in more than one sector at the same time. For example, a street trader can offer drugs as well as legal goods for sale. Even in such a case it is still important to discriminate between the different kinds of activities for policy purposes.

1.4 *Structure of the Book*

Having put the UIS into the broad context of Informal Economic Activity the next chapter will tackle the difficult question of how to define it and, having derived a working definition, will present a summary of what is known about the size of the UIS in Latin America. We shall look at socio-economic data on those who work in the UIS and examine the links between it and the Urban Formal Sector (UFS), particularly during the difficult period of the debt crisis of the 1980s, when many countries in Latin America suffered severe cuts in the rate of expansion of employment within the modern sectors of their economies.

Chapter 3 will focus on a number of social and economic problems facing those who work in the UIS, including the absence of formal social protection (in the form of pensions, social security or unemployment benefits), housing problems, problems of obtaining access to credit and to training, and the issue of gender in the UIS.

Given the historical evolution of the UIS and various evaluations of its current position and potential growth, Chapter 4 will speculate on the future of the UIS in Latin America. Does it represent the missing engine of growth in Latin America, as Hernando de Soto believes, or is its role mainly to soak up the labour that is surplus to the needs of the UFS and hence to provide a means of surviving in the cities for those outside the formal system?

2 The Urban Informal Sector: What is it and how large is it?

2.1 *Introduction*

All theories are abstractions from and simplifications of reality that ignore many phenomena that seemingly are irrelevant to the problem at hand. Progress in a subject often occurs when the theory is expanded to include at least some of the factors that have hitherto been ignored. This process of expansion describes very well the development of the concept of the UIS in the work of development economists. In much of the work of economists after World War II, such as that of Nobel prizewinner Arthur Lewis, analysis concentrated on a 'duality' between the industrial (modern, capitalist, urban) sector and the agricultural (traditional, subsistence, rural) sector (Lewis, 1954). The emphasis in development theory was on 'import substituting industrialisation' and the transfer of resources from the rural to the urban industrial sector. While economists had noticed that employment in the modern sector or unemployment were not the only options available in the urban sector, these other activities were largely ignored and they played no part in the influential 'dualist' model that Harris and Todaro (1970) put forward to explain the migratory flow from the rural to the urban sectors in developing countries. However, one exception is Reynolds (1969), who presented a model that contained two urban sectors, one of which (the trade service sector) was described as 'the multitude of people whom one sees thronging the city streets, sidewalks and back alleys in the LDCs: the petty traders, street vendors, coolies and porters, small artisans, messengers, barbers, shoe-shine boys and personal servants' (p. 91).

The two sectors in the Harris–Todaro model were the Rural (Traditional) Sector and the Urban (Modern) Sector. Workers in the Rural Sector had the choice of working in that sector for the going rural wage, W_R, or migrating to the city in the hope of obtaining a job in the Modern Sector, which paid a wage, W_M,

17

that was higher than W_R. However, the number of jobs in the Modern Sector was limited and the migrant might be unlucky, having to spend a period of unemployment while searching for a Modern Sector job. Hence, when deciding whether to migrate or not, the Rural Sector worker had to take into account the probability of getting a job in the city. What determined the decision was not W_M, but the *expected* Modern Sector wage, which is W_M multiplied by the probability of getting a job. Given the limited number of Modern Sector jobs, the probability of getting one decreased as the level of migration increased and equilibrium in the model was achieved when the expected Modern Sector wage equalled the Rural Sector wage, as in that case there would be no financial gain to be obtained by migrating.

The anthropologist, Keith Hart, is generally credited with introducing the term 'the informal sector' (Hart 1973) and this was term taken up by the International Labour Office (ILO). The report of the ILO mission to Kenya (ILO 1972) contained the first explicit discussion of the UIS and the concept greatly influenced the work of the ILO in its World Employment Programme (WEP), as well as modifying economic analysis of labour markets in developing countries.

Soon after the publication of the ILO's Kenya Report, a number of economists, in particular Fields (1975) and Mazumdar (1975, 1976a, b), extended the Harris–Todaro model to incorporate the UIS. In the model proposed by Fields (1975), the rural worker could either work for the going rural wage, W_R, or migrate and hope to find a job in the Modern (Formal) Sector at the higher wage, W_F. Given the number of such jobs was limited, the worker might not be lucky and the migrant then had two possibilities. The first was to be unemployed and search full-time for a Formal Sector job. The second was to find some kind of work in the Informal Sector at a wage W_I while searching part-time for a Formal Sector job. In the context of this model, the UIS was a 'staging-post' on the route to a Formal Sector job, the ultimate objective of all migrants.[1]

While the emergence of the concept can be dated accurately, there have been disagreements from the outset over how to define the UIS. The debate continues to this day and there is also dis-

---

1. As we shall see below, there is evidence that not all those working in the UIS want to work in the Urban Formal Sector and that there is some voluntary movement from the Urban Formal Sector to the UIS. To date, economists have not been able to model the dynamics of this two-way process – see Fields (1990) for a discussion of these problems.

agreement over the basic question of whether the concept is of any use at all. There have been two phases in the debate. First, during the 1970s there was considerable criticism of the 'duality' of the concept from those who argued for a continuum approach. Secondly, the work of Hernando de Soto (1986, English translation 1989) led to an expansion of interest in the UIS in Latin America, by putting forward an interpretation of the UIS that was very appealing in the neo-liberal, free market climate of that time.

Given the disagreements and the unresolved state of the debate, it is necessary to discuss the problem of defining the UIS in some detail. The discussion will be presented historically, so that the reader may see how views have changed over time (in response partly to criticisms of existing definitions, partly to alternative definitions and partly to the accumulation of empirical evidence concerning the UIS) and where the major areas of disagreement lie.

2.2 *The Definition of the UIS*

An anthropological definition

In Hart (1973), the basis for the definition of the informal sector was the *individual* and the distinction between the formal and informal sectors hinged upon whether the person was *wage earning* (formal sector) or *self-employed* (informal sector). In applying this definition to Ghana, Hart outlined a series of *activities* that were classified in terms of 'Formal income opportunities' and 'Informal income opportunities'. The former consisted of public sector and private sector wages and transfer payments (pensions and unemployment benefits), while the latter was sub-divided into legitimate and illegitimate income opportunities. The details need not concern us, except to note that there was no particular stress on urban activities, since among legitimate informal income opportunities were listed farming and market gardening – not activities much in evidence in urban Latin America.

By including criminal activities, such as receiving stolen goods, prostitution, bribery, political corruption, protection rackets, petty theft, burglary and armed robbery, and confidence tricks, Hart's definition differs from that developed by the ILO, which explicitly excludes criminal activities (see Sethuraman (1981), p. 14, note 4). As was argued in the previous chapter, even if an individual is involved in both legal and illegal activities, there is a strong case for analysing the activities separately and excluding criminal activities from the definition of the UIS.

19

The view of the ILO in Geneva

In contrast with Hart's emphasis on the individual and a list of activities, the ILO's Kenya Report (ILO 1972) concentrated on the *activity* and produced a list of contrasting characteristics for the formal and urban informal sectors. These are presented in Table 2.1.

Table 2.1 *The ILO Definition of the Urban Informal Sector (1972)*

	Informal sector	Formal sector
A	Ease of entry	Difficult entry
B	Reliance on indigenous resources	Frequent reliance on overseas resources
C	Family ownership of enterprises	Corporate ownership
D	Small scale of production	Large scale of operation
E	Labour intensive and adapted technology	Capital-intensive and often imported technology
F	Skills acquired outside the formal schooling system	Formally acquired skills, often expatriate
G	Unregulated and competitive markets	Protected markets (through tariffs, quotas and trade licenses)

Source: ILO (1972), p. 6.

Although the report describes these characteristics as relating to activities, within an economic context they clearly relate to *enterprises* and *markets* rather than to activities. To be made operational, these characteristics need to be translated into specific rules, such as the size that divides small-scale from large-scale enterprises, and some of the characteristics, such as the distinction between easy and difficult entry, are hard to pin down. A further problem is that it is unclear whether an activity must possess all or only some of these characteristics to be classified as belonging to the UIS.

In the event, the Report did not use the characteristics defined in Table 2.1 in its empirical work and there is no discussion of what activities were classified as being in the UIS. The estimates of the size of the UIS in Nairobi that the Report presents are therefore extremely crude.

Sethuraman (1976, p. 81) was more explicit and interpreted the ILO (1972) classification as relating to enterprises, rather than to activities. He began by identifying five activities in which informal enterprises were likely to be found:

- Manufacturing
- Construction
- Transport
- Trade
- Services

He then proposed that an enterprise in manufacturing should be regarded as 'informal' if one or more of the following conditions is met:

1. It employs 10 persons or less (including part-time and casual workers).

2. It operates on an illegal basis, contrary to the government regulations.

3. Members of the household of the head of the enterprise work in it.

4. It does not observe fixed hours/days of operation.

5. It operates in a semi-permanent or temporary structure or in a shifting location.

6. It does not use electricity in the manufacturing process.

7. It does not depend on formal financial institutions for its credit needs.

8. Its output is normally distributed directly to the final consumer.

9. Almost all those working in it have fewer than six years of formal schooling.

21

For the other four activities, the relevant characteristics are selected from 1 to 5, with additional characteristics being added for particular activities.

This classification is not derived from any conceptual model and the list seems to be designed to act as a set of fences to steer small enterprises into the corral labelled 'urban informal sector', though some large enterprises (such as Marks & Spencer) might be captured by 3 on the list.

Further, the ILO's concentration on *enterprises* makes it difficult to see what kinds of economic activities are likely to be found in the UIS. However, given the great diversity that exists between cities in different continents and in countries in different states of development, it is not obvious that this lack of specificity about activities can be avoided.

However, this definition is certainly operational and, by collecting information on the relevant characteristics of small enterprises, one could use it to classify them into the formal or informal sectors. This list (or variants of it) was the basis for many empirical studies of the UIS carried out by the ILO, some of which will be discussed in the next section.

In surveying the research that had been done on the UIS, Sethuraman (1981, p. 16) acknowledged the problems of using multiple criteria to filter enterprises because 'each criterion can be used to define a universe of its own. Consequently one is not certain about the universe to which the term informal sector refers'. He stressed the importance of employment in discriminating between enterprises and suggested that '[p]erhaps the distinguishing feature between the informal sector unit and the small enterprise is their orientation: whereas the former is motivated *primarily* by employment creation, the latter is concerned *primarily* with profit maximisation' (p. 17, italics in the original). Sethuraman's final attempt to define the UIS was that it 'consists of small-scale units engaged in the production and distribution of goods and services with the primary objective of generating employment and incomes to their participants notwithstanding the constraints on capital, both physical and human, and knowhow' (p. 17).

Sethuraman (1976, p. 70) points out that it is not only economists who have regarded the urban economy in many developing countries as having a dualistic nature and quotes McGee (1973, p. 138) as writing that most cities of the Third World can be seen as 'consisting of two juxtaposed systems of production – one derived from capitalist forms of production, the other from the peasant system of production'. He also cites Geertz (1963), who described the two systems as the 'firm-centred economy' and the 'bazaar-type economy', and Santos (1979) who referred to them as 'upper' and 'lower' circuits.

The ILO in Latin America: the view of PREALC [2]

While the ILO, through the influential work of Sethuraman, put the emphasis on the enterprise, the approach of researchers at PREALC focused on the labour market. The view was that the existence of the UIS resulted from a combination of high levels of rural to urban migration and a slow expansion of productive employment, causing an excess supply of labour for the formal sector. Hence, 'a considerable proportion of this growing labour force had no alternative but to create low-productivity jobs for itself' (Souza and Tokman, 1976, p. 355). Informal activities were undertaken as an alternative to open unemployment since, in the absence of social security benefits, individuals could not afford to be unemployed.

In its early empirical studies, PREALC used two alternative definitions to classify those working in the UIS. The first was based on household surveys and defined the UIS to include:

- domestic servants
- casual workers
- own-account (i.e. self-employed) workers
- all persons (employers, employees, hired workers and family workers) working in enterprises employing four or fewer persons.[3]

The alternative definition identified informality with low productivity and low income and included in the UIS individuals with incomes below some minimum level, usually the legal minimum wage (see Souza and Tokman, 1976).

Identifying the UIS with the poor is unhelpful, since data on income distribution for a number of countries suggest that not all

---

2. The ILO's WEP regional office for Latin America and the Caribbean was located in Santiago (Chile) and known as PREALC from the acronym of its Spanish title (*Programa Regional del Empleo para América Latina y el Caribe*). It ceased to operate under that title in December 1993 after 25 years of operation.
3. References to 'person' or 'worker' relate to individuals in the EAP, but the age range for the EAP varies both among countries and over time within individual countries. Thus in 1970 the lower age limit varied from six years of age in Peru to fifteen in Venezuela, and in Venezuela changed from ten years of age in 1950 to fifteen in 1970.

those in the UIS are poor and that some workers in the UFS are poor. Further attempts to define the UIS by criteria other than the characteristics of the activity, enterprise or labour market condition, such as identifying the UIS with the population living in slum or squatter areas or the migrant population, are criticised in Sethuraman (1976). As we shall see in Chapter 3, while many of those working in the UIS may be migrants and/or live in slums or squatter areas, not all UIS workers live in slums and some migrants work in the UFS.

While dividing the labour market into two sectors, Souza and Tokman rejected a 'dualist analytical approach' that implied that the two sectors were independent on the grounds that:

> there are links between the two, and even degrees of homogeneity. They share the same urban market, and the degree of structural heterogeneity *within* the sectors, especially the formal sector, is in any case such that it precludes the use of a single analytical category for each. The concept of a stratified formal labour market makes it possible, in fact, to view the informal sector as merely the bottom layer in the hierarchy of activities corresponding to the structural heterogeneity of the urban economy. (p. 356, italics in the original) [4]

Petty commodity production and the critics of 'dualism'

All the approaches considered so far have been based on a 'duality' between 'informal' and 'formal' sectors and, within this duality, some analysts asked whether the sectors were independent or interdependent and, if the latter, what forms the interdependence took. A number of critics of the concept of the UIS questioned the duality assumption (for example, Breman, 1985 and de Oliveira, 1985), while others, taking a Marxian perspective, have criticised the possibility of there being independent sectors.

When considering the activities carried on outside the formal sector that were the focus of the definitions discussed above, Gerry and Birkbeck (1981, p. 128) use 'petty commodity production' (PCP) when referring to 'that group of activities normally seen as lying outside the principal spheres of capitalist production

---

4. This use of the concept of the informal sector while rejecting a 'dualist' interpretation is distinctive to PREALC and distinguishes its approach from that of the ILO in Geneva.

in underdeveloped countries.' They go on to define PCP as:

> a distinct economic form, found in the context of several modes of production (feudal, capitalist or socialist). PCP is normally subordinate (though not necessarily lacking in power to take initiatives), dependent (though this does not preclude the existence of asymmetrical 'two-way functionality' between PCP and its dominant partner) and transitional (though periods of stasis and regression are always likely). (p. 128)

They argue that historically PCP:

> coexists and interpenetrates with a succession of dominant modes of production, employing the latter as the principal means of its reproduction. ... Some social formations such as Australia, New Zealand, the settler economies of Southern Africa, and the Eastern seaboard of North America have relied substantially on PCP during the initial stages of their modern development, but very quickly the rudimentary economic form has both been superseded and superseded itself within the dialectic evolution of early capitalist accumulation. (p. 128)

In the urban setting of developing countries, it is argued that petty commodity producers are tolerated by the dominant capitalist mode since they provide useful services:

> Petty commodity producers provide inputs which the capitalist firms are unable to produce profitably. These include cheap food and consumer goods for employees of capitalist firms and the state which services them, thus reducing wage costs – and inflating the salaries of managerial staff. They maintain the 'reserve army of labour', which limits the bargaining strength of organised labour, thus reducing wage costs and ensuring a flexible supply of labour to capitalist employment. They provide opportunities for additional earnings, and the possibility of establishing themselves as independent men to employees, thus both subsidising and encouraging wage employment. They provide the protected market for the products of capitalist firms. Far from being displaced by capitalism, petty commodity production, including peasant agriculture, is essential to capitalist production. (Williams and Mutebile, 1978, p. 1103)

Clearly within this framework of analysis it is not possible to think of two independent sectors, since both are part of the same overall capitalist system, although there is still a form of 'duality' in the distinction between PCP and the dominant capitalist mode. However, the 'coexistence and interpenetration' introduces a potential blurring of the demarcation line between the two categories.

Gerry and Birkbeck give an example of ice-cream sellers who may appear to be providing the same product, but be in one of three different positions in relation to the dominant mode of capitalist production. First, a *direct wage worker*, who is provided with a cart and the ice-cream by the company and paid a commission for sales. Secondly, a *disguised wage worker*, who rents a cart, but makes the ice-cream himself. Thirdly, a *self-employed worker* (or lumpen-capitalist), who makes both the cart and the ice-cream himself.

Researchers using this approach have tended to produce case studies data which, while being of considerable interest, do not specify the range of activities or occupations that should be included under the PCP heading, since these may be country and period specific. Moser (1978, 1984) provides an excellent discussion of alternative views of the UIS. Other examples of the PCP criticism of the UIS are Lewin (1985) and Birkbeck (1978, 1979). Lloyd (1982) provides an interesting discussion of the structure and dynamics of the UIS from a PCP perspective.

Other critics have focused on different issues. Roberts (1990), for example, while not rejecting the economic analysis of PREALC, links the analysis of the UIS to state regulation and provision. He argues that the informal/formal distinction is important because certain rights (to pensions, social security and other benefits) are linked to formal sector employment, so that 'the disappearance of the informal sector depends on the extension of citizenship to Latin American urban dwellers to assure basic welfare rights, not tied to employment' (p. 31). He concludes that:

... broadly defined the informal sector is the means whereby city people make out in the absence both of State provision of basic welfare services and of private mutual interest associations which defend their members and advance their interests. (Roberts, 1990, p. 35)

This definition does not specify any particular activities, but would not exclude illegal activities from the process of 'making out'. Indeed, Roberts (1990, p. 40) notes that the 'drug economy is, in certain respects, the informal sector *par excellence*'.

What this approach does focus on is the importance of the relationship between the UIS and the state and the fact that in general

26

such a relationship is missing. The absence of social security for those working in the UIS is often linked to the fact that pressure groups have ensured that pensions and social security benefits are linked to specific categories of employment in the formal sector, particularly in the benefits to those working in the public sector. Social security will be discussed in Chapter 3. The other missing linkage relates to the fact that large numbers of those working in the UIS are invisible to the state, in the sense that they do not register their economic activities with the authorities.

This opens up the possibility that part of the definition of the UIS should include legality as one of the criteria of classification. This was considered in Sethuraman (1976), who included operating 'on an illegal basis contrary to government regulations' as one of the criteria for inclusion in the UIS. Certainly the question of why so many of those working in the UIS are unregistered with the state is interesting and this was specifically addressed in the work to be discussed next.

Hernando de Soto and illegality/informality
In contrast to the arguments over the formal–informal sector 'dualism' discussed above, the formal sector hardly appears in de Soto's analysis of 'informality'. Neither is any attempt made to define the UIS explicitly, in terms either of activities or the characteristics of enterprises.

De Soto's starting point is a stylised history of Peru which focuses on rural migration to Lima, particularly since the 1940s. He notes the hostility of politicians to this migration, with various unsuccessful attempts being made to legislate against the movement of rural people to Lima or to force them to carry an entry passport. Despite this lack of legislative success in preventing rural movement to Lima, migrants who arrived found the law a problem, since:

... the greatest hostility the migrants encountered was from the legal system. Up to then, the system had been able to absorb or ignore the migrants because the small groups who came were hardly likely to upset the status quo. As the number of migrants grew, however, the system could no longer remain disinterested. When large groups of migrants reached the cities, they found themselves barred from legally established social and economic activities. It was tremendously difficult for them to acquire access to housing and an education and, above all, enter business or find a job. Quite simply, Peru's legal institutions had been developed over the years to meet the needs and

27

bolster the privileges of certain dominant groups in the cities and to isolate the peasants geographically in rural areas. As long as this system worked, the implicit legal discrimination was not apparent. Once the peasants settled in the cities, however, the law began to lose social relevance.

The migrants discovered that their numbers were considerable, that the system was not prepared to accept them, that more and more barriers were being erected against them, that they had to fight to extract every right from an unwilling establishment, that they were excluded from the facilities and benefits offered by the law, and that, ultimately, the only guarantee of their freedom and prosperity lay in their own hands. In short, they discovered that they must compete not only against people but also against the system.

Thus it was, that in order to survive, the migrants became informals. If they were to live, trade, manufacture, transport, or even consume, the cities' new inhabitants had to do so illegally. Such illegality was not antisocial in intent, like trafficking in drugs, theft, or abduction, but was designed to achieve such essentially legal objectives as building a house, providing a service, or developing a business. (de Soto, 1989a, p. 11)

It should be noted that in this crucial passage, de Soto refers to 'informals' and he makes no explicit reference to 'the informal sector'. However, as Bromley (1990) points out in a detailed analysis of the political dimensions of de Soto's approach to the informal sector, 'since his work on "informality" began to receive international publicity around 1983, he has tended to be identified as an expert on "the informal sector", and he has not directly opposed dualist divisions of the economy and the labor market'. Others have equated his 'informals' and 'informality' with 'the informal sector'. Since de Soto 'has often used the terms "the informals" and "the informal sector" virtually interchangeably', Bromley suggests that 'de Soto has effectively adopted the term "informal sector", but he has completely ignored the positivistic ILO-linked literature and definitions. Instead, he has defined the sector in his own way and using one single criterion – economic activities that contravene official regulations but that do not involve murder, theft violence, or other obvious criminal acts' (pp. 338–9) – see also Bromley (1994). This may be illustrated by the following quotation from de Soto (1989b, p. 3):

My institute in Peru has done a lot of research on the legal contraints that refer to what we call informality, i.e. the operation of basically illegal enterprises which have legal objectives. The informal sector is a euphemism for the illegal sector. We should point out, however, that their objectives are clear and honest as opposed to, say, those of the drug trade.

Having argued that the defining characteristic of informality is illegality (not criminality, but non-conformity with bureaucratic rules and regulations), de Soto provides historical case studies of the evolution of three informal activities in Lima (Informal Housing, Informal Trade and Informal Transport), before proceeding to focus on his main targets – unnecessary regulations and excessive bureaucracy. De Soto provides much anecdotal evidence to hammer home the message that the informals are the victims of bureaucracy, forced to operate illegally because of these faults in the state system.

The problem is dramatised through the account of an experiment carried out by a team from de Soto's *Instituto de Liberdad y Democracia* (ILD), which simulated the process of completing all the steps necessary to set up a small garment factory on the outskirts of Lima. They concluded that even working full time on this exercise, it would take an individual 289 days to complete the process and that the costs (including travel time, bribes and foregone profits) would be US$1,231. This example has been widely quoted in the recent literature on the informal sector, but unfortunately without a warning to the reader that a sample of one observation cannot (and should not) be used as a serious foundation for sound generalisations about the costs of bureaucracy in Peru.

The link between bureaucracy and informality is not original to de Soto. The authors of the ILO's 1972 Kenya Report in advocating 'a more positive attitude on the part of Government towards the promotion of the informal sector', recommended that the government should 'review trade and commercial licensing with a view to eliminating unnecessary licences, substitute health and safety inspection for licensing' and 'issue licences to any applicant able to pay the licence fee' (pp. 21–2).

The other strand in de Soto's message is that the high cost of bureaucracy is not borne only by those operating in the urban informal sector, but by the whole economy. The reason for this is that de Soto sees those working informally as being a potential engine for economic development. He argues that, if the regulations that prevent them from becoming formal were removed, these entrepreneurs would react in a dynamic fashion to provide a strong stimulus to growth in the economy:

In Peru, informality has turned a large number of people into entrepreneurs, into people who know how to seize opportunities by managing available resources, including their own labour, relatively efficiently. ... This new business class is a very valuable resource: it is the human capital essential for economic takeoff. (de Soto 1989a, p. 243)

This view of the potential 'informal' entrepreneurial talent that is waiting to be unleashed by the removal of bureaucratic rules and regulations has made de Soto's message particularly welcome to those advocating free-market policies in order to reduce state intervention and the resulting market distortions from the formal sector; his arguments suggest that in addition to these distortions, the 'informals' are also being held back and prevented from making their full entrepreneurial contribution to the economy.

A critique of de Soto's identification of 'informality' with 'illegality' will be presented in the Conclusions to this section. One question that arises in the light of de Soto's emphasis on 'entrepreneurs' is whether he sees all those working in the UIS as part of this potential human capital for growth, or whether he is writing only about those who are already entrepreneurs in the UIS. This point is not addressed directly in de Soto (1989a).

A hidden political agenda?

In his Introduction to the 1978 *World Development* Special Issue on the UIS, Bromley (1978a) speculated on the reasons why the UIS became so important in the debate that followed the ILO Kenya Report of 1972. His suggestions were that:

The intellectual validity of the concept was, for many people, secondary to its policy implications. It provided the rationale for the sorts of policies which the mainstream international development community wished to recommend to Kenya and other Third World countries. In other words, the informal sector concept was adopted because it arose through effective communications channels at a convenient moment, and because it embodied policy implications which were convenient for international organizations and politically middle-of-the-road governments. Support of the informal sector appeared to offer the possibility of 'helping the poor without any major threat to the rich', a potential compromise between pressures for the redistribution of income and wealth and the desire for stability on the part of economic and political elites. The very haste with which the informal sector concept was accepted by the ILO, and the remarkable speed with which many of the relevant international reports were prepared, help to explain why the concept had so many inconsistencies and anomalies in its early formulations and hence why such a diverse and inconsistent literature has arisen on the urban informal sector. (pp. 1036–7)

Bromley suggested that part of the explanation for the widespread discussion of the informal/formal dualism was undoubtedly its adoption by the ILO, but argued that more important were the interrelationships between policy discussions of the UIS and other discussions of objectives such as 'Redistribution with Growth', 'Basic needs', 'the Urban Crisis' or 'Reaching the Poorest of the Poor'.

Each of these subject areas ('labels' or 'slogans' might be a more appropriate description) provides a convenient battle-ground for a set of conflicting ideologies and interpretations of the development process, and the informal/formal dualism is simply another stage on which the same debates can be acted out. Fundamentally, these debates are between liberal, neo-classical evolutionary views that policies can be formulated to bring the 'benefits of development' to the poor, and radical, neo-Marxist views which often lead to the conclusion that only sharp (and often – some would say necessarily – violent) change can improve the situation of the poor in Third World countries. (p. 1037)

Bromley (1990, p. 337) suggests that: 'By the late 1970s, the debates about the utility of the informal sector concept had already developed into a dialogue of the deaf in which more and more was written, but apparently very little was seriously read'. Whether or not what was written was read, there has been very little genuine debate between those holding different views. Thus researchers using the ILO approach continued to collect data and ignored or played down the criticisms raised in the 1978 Special Issue. For example, Sethuraman (1981, p. 19) does refer, briefly, to the 1978 Special Issue, but rejects the criticisms of the dualist approach presented there on the grounds that they are based on 'the mistaken notion that dualism denies the presence of interdependence between the two subsectors'.

One explanation of why dualists and anti-dualists have failed to engage in meaningful debate may be the increasing degree of specialisation within the social sciences, so that more and more of those who practise one discipline, such as economics, look inward

31

and ignore the work of those in other disciplines that is not couched in the language of their chosen field.

Peattie (1987), who is critical of the fuzziness of the concept of the informal sector, suggests that its continuing popularity results from its usefulness to different groups of analysts:

> The concept of an 'informal sector' is coming into more and more general use because it appears to serve the purposes of many different groups with a number of different – even conflicting – purposes. It appeals to liberals with an interest in problems of poverty; to economic planners who want their accounting systems to represent the actual economy more accurately; to radicals who want to bring into planning analysis a more structuralist view of the economy; and to those who would like to 'privatize' activities such as housing production, either out of a populist commitment to action by 'the people' or out of conservative commitment to restraint in government welfare expenditures.
>
> But it serves all these groups as a banner. It serves none of them adequately as a tool of analysis or as a framework for development policy. (p. 857)

Not all writers accepted the criticism that the fuzziness of the UIS was necessarily a problem, see Chandavarkar (1988) and Khundker (1988). The latter points out that:

> [t]he notion of 'class' has a good theoretical definition, but it has nevertheless proved problematic to assign people into different classes, or to ascribe to them their class views. Yet Marxists have not been able to abandon the term precisely because of its usefulness in explaining many, if not all, aspects of reality. (p. 1264)

While one may sympathise with her criticisms of the fuzziness of the concept of the UIS and agree with her rejection of the identification of the UIS with poverty, one may disagree with her criticisms of those who seek to measure the size of the UIS. While it has not been possible to obtain agreement for a theoretical definition of the UIS that is completely general, it may yet be possible to define the UIS in a particular country sufficiently clearly to make the collection of useful data possible. By avoiding the temptation to treat the UIS as a homogeneous sector and collecting data in disaggregated form, so that the different actors and activities within the sector can be identified, one may encompass the position advocated by Peattie:

Accounting should not, in any event, be an end in itself; let us rather identify which questions of policy we wanted the accountants to serve, and then look at the problems of data-collection within the context of those questions, rather than trying to gather some sort of all-purpose 'data base' on a fuzzy category. (1987, p. 858)

This would suggest carrying out specific studies to collect empirical information after particular policy questions have been raised rather than the routine ongoing collection of statistical data across a wide range of formal and informal activities. The former method has its advantages in terms of clarity of focus, but one-off studies do not provide much information on the generality, if any, or the dynamics of the situation being investigated. For example, how would the findings of a specific study be affected by economic growth or recession? This kind of question requires long-term data collected using the second approach. The ideal solution is to carry out the analysis using both approaches.

Those critics who have argued that there was a hidden agenda behind the rapid acceptance of the UIS concept have focused on an important point that needs to be borne in mind. However, it can still be argued that the ILO is correct in its efforts to define the UIS and make its regular measurement part of the duties of national income statisticians on the grounds that, if the data are available in sufficiently disaggregate form, they will provide an important input into any policy debate, regardless of the agenda of the parties to the debate.

Conclusions

Having surveyed the main efforts to define the UIS the time has come to attempt an evaluation and, perhaps, a reconciliation of the different positions. This task is not easy, as in some cases we are dealing with *prescriptive*, rather than *descriptive* definitions, whether it be the attempt to delineate the range of activities available to the poor to 'make out in the city' or the historical process of capitalist development that characterises petty commodity production.

Dualism and interdependence. The author would argue that the ILO/PREALC definitions are aimed at the operational target of measurement and policy analysis and, while the question of a sharp division between the formal and informal sectors remains difficult to resolve in terms of a completely general definition in the abstract, there is no reason why one cannot attempt to specify the appropriate grouping for any country without aiming for a definition that assumes that the UIS and UFS are independent. The author accepts this position on the grounds that, while it may not be intellectually neat and tidy, the concept of the UIS is not so fuzzy or subjective that it cannot be usefully applied to illuminate many aspects of the urban labour market and the policy issues that arise. The quantitative discussion that follows will make use of data produced by PREALC, augmented by other studies that use consistent definitions of the UIS.

The PCP criticism of 'dualism' in the work of the ILO and others has two strands; first that the distinction between formal and informal is an arbitrary one in a capitalist continuum and, secondly, that the two sectors cannot be independent. The first objection seems less than convincing when one notes that the PCP argument itself makes use of the distinction between PCP and the dominant mode of capitalist production. While this distinction involves a dialectic evolution, *at a point of time*, it should be possible to specify what is PCP and what represents the dominant mode. It would be interesting to see how the listing of activities corresponding to PCP would differ from that obtained using the concept of the UIS.

The second criticism is only valid where claims of independence have been made. The concept of the UIS requires that the two categories 'formal' and 'informal' should be exhaustive and mutually exclusive and that it is possible to discriminate between them (in order to categorise the agents to be classified), but logically it does not require them to be independent (i.e. non-interactive). In the next section, we shall examine the links between the UIS and the UFS and show that the two sectors are neither independent nor autonomous in their actions.

Informality and illegality. Reconciling the views of the ILO and PREALC with those of de Soto is not difficult over questions of definition, since de Soto does not put forward an explicit definition of the UIS. However, there are differences between de Soto and PREALC over the direction of causality between informality and illegality. For de Soto it is the *effect* of bureaucratic restrictions forcing small enterprises to become illegal that is the cause of the UIS, but for PREALC poverty is the *cause* of the UIS and illegality/informality is a *consequence* of the situation under which enterprises operate in the UIS. Thus Tokman (1990, pp. 107–8) wrote:

34

The traditional interpretation of the informal sector in Latin America has been one of marginalisation. The diagnosis attributed the situation mainly to insufficient job creation in modern activities. Hence, the labour surplus occupied in the informal sector was considered a marginal population. As such, their expectations were to move away to modern activities and while this objective became increasingly difficult to attain, the result was growing political antagonism and resentment. A more recent approach to informal activities postulates that, contrary to the common belief, the informal workers are truly capitalist entrepreneurs in developing countries. They have shown a capacity to manage businesses in highly unfavourable situations. Their capacity to grow is conditioned by State intervention, mostly through excessive legal requirements and protection of markets for more formal endeavours. The promotion of private initiative through deregulation at this petty capitalist level is the prescription associated to this interpretation.

There are no easy answers to complex development problems. There is always the attraction of searching for what McKee (1988) describes as 'the missing piece strategy'. That is to identify a single constraint which, when removed, will allow a more productive and profitable livelihood of the beneficiaries. At the macro-level the most popular 'missing piece' is excessive or inadequate State regulations and bureaucratic interventions. At the micro-level, the most common is access to credit. This strategy is also attractive because of the expected automaticity of the effects. In practice, while both interventions are necessary components of a more comprehensive package, taken in isolation they will only produce partial and in many instances, marginal results. Inadequate regulation is a consequence and not a cause of informal production.

Research carried out since the publication of de Soto (1989a) suggests that the equating 'formal/informal' with 'legal/illegal' may be an oversimplification and there are also difficulties in defining what constitutes high or low bureaucratic barriers for 'informals' – (see Box 2.1 below). This limits the usefulness of de Soto's approach to defining (and measuring the size of) the UIS. However, while his contribution may be more demagogic than pedagogic, de Soto has put the case for the 'informal' and spotlighted examples of excessive bureaucracy in Peru. Whether a general call for the reduction of the state follows from this approach (or is desirable) is a subject we shall return to in Chapter 4.

Box 2.1 The Links between Informality and Illegality

In his analysis of the 'informals' in Lima, Hernando de Soto argues that it is the high level of bureaucracy, with its accompanying burden of rules and restrictions, that drive people to operate informally and illegally. This suggests two important hypotheses: (i) there is a direct correspondence between the two dichotomies 'formal/informal' and 'legal/illegal' and (ii) the size of the informal sector is related to the degree of bureaucracy – the greater the amount of bureaucratic regulation, the larger the number of 'informals' will be. However, research on the UIS casts some doubt on both these propositions.

(i) Formal/informal *versus* legal/illegal. Tokman (1992, Chapter 1) suggests that the equation of formal/informal and legal/illegal is an oversimplification and presents evidence from a 1990 survey of enterprises in Mexico in 1990 showing that a majority of them were neither illegal nor fully legal. In the survey, 27.3% were classified as being underground (i.e. having no registration), 18.2% were of restricted illegality (i.e. having some registration at no cost or requiring only a once-for-all payment), 36.4% were of restricted legality (i.e. having all the required registrations, but not contributing to all of them) and only 18.2% of the enterprises were classified as being legal (i.e. meeting all requirements and making all the necessary contributions). There is clearly a spectrum of positions, with 'legal' and 'illegal' merely being the two extremes.

This study showed some interesting differences by sector: in Manufacturing industry, a majority of enterprises were illegal (46.1% underground and 23.1% of restricted illegality); in Commerce, all the enterprises were in an intermediate position (25% of restricted illegality and 75% of restricted legality), while in Services, all the enterprises had some degree of legality (80% of restricted legality and 20% legal). There were also differences with respect to location: a majority of shops were legal (36.4% of restricted legality and 27.3% legal), while a majority of those operating from home were illegal (55.6% underground and 11.1% of restricted illegality). These patterns suggest that visibility may have a good deal to do with the position the enterprise chooses in the spectrum.

(ii) The degree of bureaucracy and the size of the UIS. Tokman (1992, Chapter 1) also presents data on the number of steps involved in completing registration, a figure that represents one dimension of the degree of bureaucracy. For Bolivia, five steps are involved in the process of registration, while in Ecuador, the number is 60.

Continued

Given the relative numbers of restrictions, one might expect there to be much less illegality in Bolivia than in Ecuador. However, this seems not to be the case. Bolivia: Casanovas (1992) reports that a Tax Reform Law enacted in Bolivia in 1987 greatly simplified the registration process in order to encourage 'all natural persons and legal entities subject to VAT' to be listed on a Single National Register of Taxpayers (RUC). Within this Register was a Simplified Tax Regime that was intended for the UIS.

The simplification may have had a positive effect, as during the first ten months 'almost half of Bolivia's informal businesses fulfilled their obligation to register for tax purposes. This shows a political will on the part of the informal sector to comply with the legal regulations in force [... but d]espite this initial determination, only 19.04 percent of all those registered in the RUC paid their taxes in the last two-month period under review, and this proportion reaches only 9.37 percent when compared to the number of taxpayers in the estimated total of informal businesses in the major cities.' (p. 43). One element here seems to be the degree of enforcement and Casanovas reports that only about 35% of mobile stall-holders in La Paz paid the daily tax, as required by the Municipal authorities, to the eighteen collectors operating in that large city.

Ecuador: In a study of nearly 300 small enterprises in Ecuador in 1990, Klein and Tokman (1993) found that 28% were underground, 58% were of restricted legality/illegality and only 14% were completely legal. One interesting finding was that despite the complexity of registration, 69% of enterprises had completed at least the initial registration, a process that involved 39 steps. Of these, 34 are required for an individual to become registered as a 'craftsman' and this process is expensive both in terms of time and money. Why bother, since the individual is not pressured to do so? The answer lies in the tax benefits to be obtained after registration as a craftsman; (i) with respect to personal income tax, there is a 60% discount on income derived from profits on crafts and (ii) all products made and sold by craftsmen are exempt from VAT (see Lagos, 1992).

These case studies suggest two important conclusions:

1. The identification of 'formal/informal' with 'legal/illegal' is clearly a considerable oversimplification; the reality seems much greyer than the legal/illegal dichotomy suggests with partial-legality being the norm in many Latin American countries.

2. The effect of bureaucracy on the UIS cannot be gauged simply by looking at the degree of complexity or its apparent size. The evidence suggests that individuals weigh up the costs and benefits of compliance (or non-compliance) with regulations and act rationally given the constraints and the rewards.

The Mexican study reported in Box 2.1 is based on a relatively small sample of 22 enterprises. However, results are available in Contreras and Thomas (1994) from a sample of over 400 small enterprises (over the size range one person, two to four persons and five to nine persons) in Santiago (Chile) in November 1992. Approximately equal numbers of enterprises were drawn from four activities (garment making, equipment repairs, furniture making and food preparation and selling). Across the whole sample it was found that 46 per cent were illegal, 22 per cent were of restricted legality (i.e. combining the two restricted categories discussed above) and 32 per cent were legal. There were some notable differences across activities; there was a higher degree of legality in equipment repairs than in the other activities and, in general, a higher proportion of the largest enterprises were legal than were own-account workers. The biggest concentration of illegality was among women garment makers who worked at home, presumably because this group had little contact with officialdom and regulations.

To end this discussion of the problems of defining the UIS, we must conclude that this is not an area for the purist. We have not emerged from this investigation with a definition of the UIS that is derived from an agreed theoretical or conceptual starting point and which can be applied uniformly across all countries. I would argue that there is little to be gained through further definitional disputation, since no single definition will satisfy all analysts of the UIS.

In the context of Latin America, the work of the researchers at PREALC at least provides an approach that recognises the characteristics of the region. They have built up a consistent collection of data over the years and, by using their definition and the statistical material they have collected, we are able to analyse and monitor changes in the UIS in Latin America over a long period of time. These and other data on the UIS in Latin America will be presented in the next section.[5]

---

5. For further readings on the definition of the UIS, see Connolly (1985, 1990), Sanyal (1988), Scott (1979), Thomas (1990/91), Thorp (1990), Tokman (1978a, b, 1989, 1991) and Uzzell (1980).

2.3 *The Size of the UIS*

The question of how to measure the UIS raises a number of new issues concerning *what* is to be measured and *how* is it to be measured. The first question takes us back to the need to specify what is to be included in the UIS and, when this has been settled, we have to decide what variables are to be collected and how to collect them.

Starting from the PREALC definition of the UIS as presented in Souza and Tokman (1976), there are three main components:

Own-account workers
It seems clear that own-account workers (other than professionals, such as doctors, lawyers and architects) are not directly part of the formal sector and they will constitute an important component of the UIS in any country. In some studies, such workers are described as casual workers, though in many cases casual workers may be working for others and need to be classified accordingly.

Domestic servants
Domestic servants would also seem to represent another important group within the UIS, as was assumed in Souza and Tokman (1976), on the grounds that domestic service was often the route into the labour market for female migrants to the city who did not have the skills to find employment in the formal sector. However, more recently there has been a change of attitude on the part of the ILO and PREALC towards the inclusion of domestic servants in the UIS. Thus Mezzera (1989, p. 52) argues that:

> For two reasons PREALC analysts have concluded that domestic servants should not be included in the informal sector. The first is theoretical: the informal sector is a set of productive units, not of people, and an individual who works in domestic service is not a productive unit, but a wage-earner who generally depends on income from the modern sector. The second reason is empirical: including domestic service in the informal sector introduces an enormous conceptional bias of the informal sector in favor of the personal characteristics of this particular group, which is quite large and homogeneous. The vast majority are women, particularly unskilled young women who are migrants and wage-earners with low incomes and long working hours. The result is that the informal sector becomes

39

identified with unskilled women who are migrants and wage-earners who have no relationship to microenterprises.

Haan (1989a, p. 8), in explaining the Geneva ILO's approach as it moves towards international agreement on how the UIS will be measured for inclusion in the National Income Accounts, argues that:

> At the same time, there are good reasons to *exclude* domestic servants from the informal sector in spite of their 'ease of entry': domestic servants generally have fixed salaries (with sometimes even a formal contract and coverage of social security) and do not own any capital equipment but make use of the (usually modern) household appliances of their employer.

Some observers might disagree with these views, on the grounds that domestic service is one of the classic routes for migrant women to enter the labour force and that there is frequently rather less formality in contractual arrangements than Haan suggests. However, the arguments for separating domestic service from UIS activities have some merits, since for policy purposes it may be important to treat domestic servants as a separate group. Policies that are directed towards the UIS need to focus on the economic operations of producing and selling goods and services and the needs of those involved, such as access to training and credit. The needs of domestic servants may not be the same. For example, if in general they are not as well cared for as Haan believes, the answer may be special legislation to deal with this particular case.

Fortunately, PREALC has published data separately on the number of domestic servants, the numbers of self-employed and the number of small enterprises, so one can construct estimates of the size of the informal sector combining these groups if one so wishes. This is what was done by PREALC in the data presented in Table 2.3 below. This illustrates the advantages of preparing data in a disaggregate form, so that the components are available to be used in combinations appropriate for analysing particular problems.

Small enterprises
The third important group are small enterprises employing less than some minimum number of employees, either as wage earners or as unpaid family labour. The minimum number chosen varies among countries, but is usually either five or ten. The choice

depends mainly on institutional factors, such as the minimum size at which enterprises have to register, comply with industrial regulations and/or satisfy other formal requirements. Where information is available on the characteristics of the enterprise which enable it to be classified into 'formal' or 'informal', the total number of small enterprises can be disaggregated into those in the UIS and those in the UFS. However, when such information is not available, it is only possible to present data on the total number of small enterprises. In such cases, it is best to publish data on own-account workers and small enterprises separately, since it would be misleading to present data based on the sum of the two groups as an estimate of the size of the UIS; the resulting estimate would be biased upwards by the number of small enterprises that should properly be classified as being in the UFS.

Given agreement over what groups constitute the UIS, the next question is what do we wish to measure? One obvious answer is the size of the UIS, but what do we mean by size? The first possibility is that size equals the number of persons working in the UIS and, since this involves a head-count, it is the easiest dimension of size to measure. A relatively simple set of questions is sufficient to obtain information to determine whether individuals are self-employed and their branches of economic activity, and to eliminate professionals (such as doctors, lawyers, academics, etc.) from the informal sector. Similarly, one would need to apply the criteria discussed in the previous section to allocate small enterprises between the UIS and the UFS.

It is also important to collect information on whether individuals have a secondary occupation, since there is some evidence (mainly anecdotal) that some workers from the formal sector 'moonlight' in the informal sector. One example is said to involve public servants, who in the evenings or at weekends use their cars to operate as unofficial taxi-drivers. The problems of estimating the numbers of such part-time informal sector workers is discussed in Rossini and Thomas (1990).

An alternative is that size is defined in terms of the value of the output of the UIS (possibly measured as a percentage of the level of measured GNP), but this is more difficult. First, it is necessary to obtain information about the output of goods and services produced by individuals or enterprises in order to discover in which economic activities they are operating. Then it is necessary to obtain information on the costs of production and the prices charged for these goods and services in order to produce estimates of the money values of the goods and services that can then be aggregated to form an overall estimate of the value added by the informal sector.

Given the difficulties of data collection and estimation, it is perhaps not surprising that very little research of this kind has been reported. One study that does provide data for Peru is Carbonetto and Carazo (1986, p. 25), where it is reported that in 1981 the UIS (defined to include domestic servants) constituted 32.1 per cent of the non-agricultural EAP. Despite representing a large source of employment for the urban labour force, the value of the output of the UIS was only 8.2 per cent of the total output of the Non-agricultural EAP. Villarán (1993, p. 162) provides disaggregate data on the industrial sector in Peru in 1987 and reports that artisans or craft-workers represented 23 per cent of the EAP in this sector and produced 5 per cent of the GNP of the sector. Micro-firms (employing between one and five workers) were 29 per cent of the EAP and produced 8 per cent of GNP. Small firms (with five to nineteen employees) constituted 19 per cent of the EAP and produced 13 per cent of industrial GNP. Medium-sized firms (employing between 20 and 199 workers) were 16 per cent of the industrial EAP and produced 28 per cent of the sector's GNP, while large firms (employing over 200 workers and with an average size of almost 450 workers per firm) represented 13 per cent of the EAP, but produced 46 per cent of the GNP. Clearly, the UIS is characterised by high levels of employment coupled with very low levels of productivity.

There is general agreement that the most satisfactory way to collect data on the UIS is through household surveys, since they offer the most complete coverage and enable researchers to identify and enumerate homeworkers and itinerant workers, two important groups that are difficult to locate through surveys of establishments. One approach that could identify and quantify the different types of occupations and activities within the UIS would be to combine a household survey with a follow-up survey of enterprises identified through the household survey. This approach was the basis for the large-scale survey of the UIS in Lima that is summarised in Thomas (1992a), Chapter 4.

The nine case studies of the UIS in selected cities in Africa, Asia and Latin America presented in Sethuraman (1981) illustrate very clearly the problems of sample design. Six of the nine were based on surveys of enterprises – Freetown (Sierra Leone), Lagos (Nigeria), Kano (Nigeria), Kumasi (Ghana), Colombo (Sri Lanka) and Manilla (the Philippines), while the remaining three were based on household surveys – Jakarta (Indonesia), Cordoba (Argentina) and

Campinas (Brazil). In summarising the general findings across the studies, Sethuraman noted that:

> Female participation in the informal sector seems surprisingly small. The proportion of women participating in this sector was: 25 per cent in Freetown; 11 per cent in Kano; 15 per cent in Lagos; 12 per cent in Colombo; 25 per cent in Jakarta; 38 per cent in Cordoba and 12 per cent in Campinas. In Manila, however, 57 per cent of the entrepreneurs, mostly in trade, were females. Though, in some cases, female participation seems to be underestimated owing to sampling design, dominance of males in the informal sector is, in general, noticeable in Africa, Asia and Latin America. In specific activities, notably in trade and domestic service, female participation is significantly higher than in others. (p. 190)

Even though Sethuraman admits that sample design may have biased the results and omits Kumasi (which focused only on selected activities that are likely to be male preserves – manufacturing and repairs), it is misleading to compare the results of these studies. In addition to being a mixture of household and enterprise surveys, some were random samples while others used predetermined quotas for enterprises in industry, commerce and services. Clearly great care must be taken when evaluating comparisons based on studies using different sampling designs.

During the 1970s, the ILO carried out a large number of studies of the UIS in cities in Africa, Asia and Latin America. By the 1980s, however, interest in the question of measurement seems to have decreased on the part of researchers at the ILO in Geneva.[6] Fortunately for those interested in the UIS in Latin America, PRE-ALC continued to study this sector and is the source of a considerable amount of data on the UIS in Latin America, with the merit that cross-country studies use a consistent definition of the UIS.

Table 2.2 presents data for the period 1950 to 1970 for the structure of the Urban Labour Force (ULF). The last row, for Latin America as a whole, suggests that there was remarkably little change over the 20 years, with the UIS remaining at a steady 20 per cent despite the process of ISI that went on during

---

6. See Sethuraman (1981) and Lubell (1991) for details of the earlier studies. It is striking that the latter book, which is concerned with the UIS in the 1980s and 1990s, contains so little empirical evidence for Africa and Asia that dates from after 1980. For an update, see ILO (1991b, 1992).

Table 2.2 *The Structure of the Urban Labour Force, 1950, 1960 and 1970 (percentage of ULF in each category)*

Country	1950			1960			1970		
	UIS	DS	FS	UIS	DS	FS	UIS	DS	FS
Argentina	13.2	7.9	78.9	11.3	7.0	81.7	11.6	7.5	80.9
Bolivia	43.6	18.7	37.7	42.4	16.7	40.9	41.4	14.6	44.0
Brazil	17.6	9.7	72.7	22.9	9.7	67.4	17.4	10.5	72.1
Chile	21.7	13.2	64.9	18.9	12.6	68.5	16.5	7.4	76.1
Colombia	21.7	17.3	61.0	23.1	14.9	62.0	20.4	11.0	68.6
Ecuador	23.2	12.0	64.8	37.3	11.8	50.9	33.5	24.4	42.1
Paraguay	—	—	—	—	—	—	—	—	—
Peru	27.2	19.7	53.1	30.8	12.3	56.9	33.7	7.3	59.0
Uruguay	11.6	7.1	81.3	12.6	7.0	80.4	13.7	7.0	79.3
Venezuela	22.3	9.8	67.9	22.3	9.4	68.3	22.4	9.0	68.6
Costa Rica	15.0	14.3	70.7	14.4	12.1	73.5	12.8	9.8	77.4
El Salvador	23.3	19.3	57.4	20.4	17.7	61.9	21.9	17.6	60.5
Guatemala	35.0	16.6	48.4	35.8	13.0	57.4	32.4	11.1	56.5
Honduras	23.8	15.9	60.3	23.6	17.6	58.8	27.5	11.2	61.3
Nicaragua	21.5	17.2	61.3	24.5	16.1	59.4	26.5	17.1	56.4
Panama	13.5	11.8	74.7	13.7	12.7	73.6	17.4	9.1	73.5
Dominican Republic	17.4	12.8	69.8	30.4	12.0	57.6	25.2	8.8	66.0
Mexico	28.1	9.3	62.6	21.9	7.7	70.4	27.8	7.1	65.1
Latin America	20.0	10.8	69.2	21.0	9.9	69.1	20.2	9.5	70.2

Source: PREALC (1982), various tables.

Key:
UIS: Urban Informal Sector, defined as own-account workers plus unpaid family workers.
DS: Domestic service.
FS: Formal sector, defined as (100–UIS–DS).

the period. The importance of the UIS varies considerably between countries, ranging in 1950 from 11.6 per cent in Uruguay
to 43.6 per cent in Bolivia, with four countries having more than
25 per cent of the ULF in the UIS. Although individual countries
show some changes over the period (for example, the UIS increased considerably in the Dominican Republic), overall the wide
differences remain in 1970, ranging from 11.6 per cent in Argentina to 41.4 per cent in Bolivia, with eight countries having more
than 25 per cent of the ULF in the UIS.

Data are presented in Table 2.3, covering the 1980s and the
difficult period of the debt crisis. They show that, for Latin
America as a whole, there was a dramatic fall in the percentage of
the ULF employed in the public sector and large private firms,
from 59.8 per cent in 1980 to 45.7 per cent in 1992. This was
offset by an increase of the percentage of small firms from 14.6
per cent in 1980 to 22.5 per cent in 1992 and own-account
workers from 19.2 per cent in 1980 to 25.0 per cent in 1992.
While not all the small firms should be included in the UIS, given
the increases in both own-account workers and small firms, it
seems safe to say that the UIS has expanded considerably during
the period.

In contrast with these large movements in own-account workers
and small firms, the percentage of Non-Agricultural Employment
in Domestic Service for Latin America changed by only a small
amount over the period. Looking at individual countries, there is
very little agreement in the movement of these three categories
and, in Costa Rica, the percentage in Domestic Service falls while
the percentages in the other two categories rises. This reinforces
the argument that data on Domestic Service should be presented
separately.

PREALC (1993) also presents data on the numbers of individuals involved that bring out the effects of population growth during
the period. Thus the decline in the percentage of the ULF in large
private firms from 44.1 per cent to 30.8 per cent and in the public
sector from 15.7 per cent to 14.9 per cent actually represented a
growth from 30 million to 32 million and from 11 million to 16
million respectively, that is a total increase of 7 million persons in
these two categories of the UFS. The change in domestic service
from 6.4 per cent to 6.9 per cent represented a growth from 4
million to 7 million. However, the changes in the other two groups
were more dramatic; the rise of the percentage of the ULF in small
firms from 14.6 per cent to 22.5 per cent resulted in an increase
from 10 million to 24 million, while the change in own-account
workers from 19.2 per cent to 25.0 per cent represented an increase

Table 2.3 *The Structure of Non-agricultural Employment in some Latin American Countries, 1980–92*

Country/ Year	Informal Sector[1]				Formal Sector		
	Own-account workers	Domestic service	Small firms	Total	Public sector	Large private firms	Total
L. America							
1980	19.2	6.4	14.6	40.2	15.7	44.1	59.8
1985	22.6	7.8	16.6	47.0	16.6	36.5	53.1
1990	24.0	6.9	21.8	52.7	15.6	31.7	47.3
1992	25.0	6.9	22.5	54.4	14.9	30.8	45.7
Argentina							
1980	20.4	6.0	13.0	39.4	18.9	41.8	60.7
1985	22.9	6.5	13.3	42.7	19.1	38.2	57.3
1990	24.7	7.9	14.9	47.5	19.3	33.2	52.5
1992	25.9	7.8	15.9	49.6	17.7	32.7	50.4
Brazil							
1980	17.3	6.7	9.7	33.7	11.1	55.2	66.3
1985	21.1	9.1	14.5	44.7	12.0	43.4	55.4
1990	21.0	7.7	23.3	52.0	11.0	36.9	47.9
1992	22.5	7.8	22.5	54.1	10.4	35.4	45.8
Chile							
1980	27.8	8.3	14.3	50.4	11.9	37.7	49.6
1985	24.4	9.8	19.1	53.3	9.9	36.8	46.7
1990	23.6	8.1	18.3	50.0	7.0	43.0	50.0
1992	23.0	7.5	19.0	49.5	8.1	42.3	50.4
Colombia							
1980	25.3	6.7	20.5	52.5	13.8	33.7	47.5
1985	28.0	7.0	20.7	55.7	12.4	31.8	44.2
1990	25.1	6.2	27.8	59.1	10.6	30.2	40.8
1992	25.4	5.9	29.0	60.3	9.9	29.6	39.5
Costa Rica							
1980	16.3	6.1	14.0	36.4	26.7	36.9	63.6
1985	17.2	6.2	17.1	40.5	26.3	33.1	59.4
1990	17.6	5.6	22.0	45.2	23.0	31.7	54.7
1992	20.9	5.8	23.0	49.7	20.9	29.4	50.3
Mexico							
1980	18.0	6.2	24.9	49.1	21.8	29.1	50.9
1985	23.5	6.4	21.4	51.3	25.5	23.2	48.7
1990	30.4	5.6	19.5	55.5	25.0	19.6	44.6
1992	30.5	5.5	20.0	56.0	24.5	19.5	44.0

	Informal Sector[1]				Formal Sector		
Country/ Year	Own- account workers	Domestic service	Small firms	Total	Public sector	Large private firms	Total
Venezuela							
1980	21.2	4.5	8.8	34.5	25.6	39.8	65.4
1985	21.3	4.9	13.7	39.9	24.5	35.6	60.1
1990	21.4	5.0	22.1	48.5	22.6	28.9	51.5
1992	22.3	5.0	23.6	50.9	20.0	29.1	49.1

Source: PREALC (1993), p. 4, Table 2.

Note 1
The label 'informal sector', defined to include own-account workers, domestic servants and small businesses, appears in the original table in PREALC (1993). Small businesses are 'those which have 5 or 10 workers, depending on the available information'.

from 13 million to 26 million. Clearly, the growth of 27 million in the number of own-account workers and persons in small firms during the period was considerably larger than the growth of 7 million in the public sector and large firms combined; indeed the increase in own-account workers alone is almost twice this number. Thus the response in Latin America to the debt crisis and structural adjustment was increased informality.

There are some interesting differences across countries, with relatively large increases in the percentage of own-account workers in Agentina, Brazil, Costa Rica and Mexico. The percentage of small firms rose significantly in Brazil, Chile, Colombia, Costa Rica and Venezuela, but fell in Mexico. The percentage of the ULF in large firms fell in all countries with the exception of Chile, where the percentage rose from 37.7 per cent to 42.3 per cent over the period, while the percentage of own-account workers fell from 27.8 per cent to 23.0 per cent.

2.4 *The Structure of the UIS*

The information in Tables 2.2 and 2.3 provides an overview of what has happened to the UIS over the past 40 years and it is clear that this sector has flourished and shows no sign of withering away. The data on total numbers, however, do not provide us with any insight into the structure of the UIS – for example, who is involved and what do they do? For such information, one must turn to a large number of studies that have analysed the characteristics of those working in the UIS.[7]

In this chapter we shall concentrate on studies that have attempted to look at the UIS at the basic level of estimating how large it is and, in general terms, who is doing what. Two examples are presented. The first, MIDEPLAN (1992), is a large-scale study of Chile that was carried out in 1990. Chile is generally regarded as having made a success of its adjustment to the crisis of the 1980s and is the only country in Table 2.3 in which the percentage of workers in large private firms grew between 1980 and 1992.

The second, IDESI (1991a–f), was carried out in Peru, a country in which the UIS is relatively more important than it is in Chile and which experienced a period of severe economic chaos in the late 1980s during the presidency of Alan García. The data refer to the UIS in seven Peruvian cities in 1989.

The Chilean study was carried out for the Ministry of Planning (MIDEPLAN) in November 1990 and involved a sample of 21,000 households (both urban and rural) throughout Chile, with an additional sample of 4,000 households in the Metropolitan Region of Santiago to obtain more detailed information on a number of questions. In this survey the UIS was defined as own-account workers, unpaid family workers, those working in manufacturing, commerce and services in firms involving five or fewer persons. The survey found that 83.4 per cent of the EAP was in non-agricultural activities and of these, 65.8 per cent were in the UFS, 26.7 per cent were in the UIS and the remaining 7.5 per cent were in domestic service.

Table 2.4 explores a number of dimensions of the UIS and UFS. For example, the data on age suggest that there is a concentration of older workers in the UIS, a result that one might expect even in a country with a relatively developed social security system. The data on education show a concentration of UIS workers with only Primary or incomplete Secondary education (68.8 per cent), as compared with the UFS (42 per cent). With respect to hours worked,

---

7. There is no shortage of information. Here PREALC (1991b) is invaluable, as it contains an annotated bibliography of 396 studies of the UIS in Latin America up to 1991, about 40 of which report some empirical information. A further listing by country of reasonably accessible studies of the UIS in Latin America is given in the Appendix to this chapter.

Table 2.4 *The Structure of UIS and UFS in Chile, 1990*

Characteristic	UIS	UFS
Sector as % of non-agricultural EAP[1]	26.7	65.8
Sex		
Female	31.4	31.7
Male	68.6	68.3
Total	100.0	100.0
Age (years) [1]		
15–24	20.6	68.5
25–34	20.7	72.7
35–44	31.3	66.0
45–54	31.9	60.4
55–64	42.9	49.7
65 or more	58.0	37.3
Education		
Primary	47.4	23.8
Secondary (incomplete)	21.4	18.2
Secondary (complete)	19.9	28.1
Higher (incomplete)	6.0	12.0
Higher (complete)	2.3	14.9
Other	3.0	3.0
Total	100.0	100.0
Hours of work		
1–4	8.3	2.5
4–8	42.3	46.1
8 or more	49.4	51.4
Total	100.0	100.0
Economic activity		
Industry	19.5	23.4
Construction	11.4	8.7
Commerce	38.4	16.1
Services	17.5	36.9
Transport	9.1	9.5
Other	4.1	5.4
Total	100.0	100.0
Place of work [2]		
In the home	18.8	11.1
Workshop next to home	17.2	11.7
Office (etc.) away from home	24.5	58.5
Deliveries, at client's home	16.4	4.0
In the streets	21.2	9.9
Other	1.9	4.8
Total	100.0	100.0

Source: MIDEPLAN (1992), p. 333, Table 7. *Notes:* 1. Percentages do not total 100 since categories do not include domestic service. 2. For comparability with the UIS, the comparison involves only small enterprises in the UFS.

the only obvious difference is a higher percentage in the UIS who work for four or fewer hours per day. The data on economic activity show a concentration of UIS workers in Commerce (38.4 per cent), while for the UFS, the major concentration is in Services (36.9 per cent). Finally, in relation to the place of work, there are large differences between the percentages working in or adjacent to the home (36.0 per cent in UIS versus 22.8 per cent in the UFS), those working in a fixed location away from the home, such as an office (24.5 per cent in the UIS versus 58.5 per cent in the UFS) and those working in the streets (21.2 per cent in the UIS versus 9.9 per cent in the UFS).

The second example is presented in Table 2.5, which reports some of the preliminary results of six surveys that were carried out in 1989 in seven cities in Peru. The characteristics of the cities covered vary widely and they range geographically from Arequipa, Peru's second largest city located in the Andes to the south of Lima, to Trujillo, Peru's third largest city in the desert far to the north of Lima. Also included are Cuzco – the capital of the Inca Empire in pre-Columbian days, Puno and Juliaca – situated on the antiplano near Lake Titicaca, Ica – a small town in the desert south of Lima and, finally, Iquitos – a port in the jungle on the banks of the River Amazon. The studies were commissioned by IDESI (*Instituto de Desarrollo del Sector Informal*), a Peruvian NGO that operates credit programmes for those working in the UIS. The studies have the merit that they were based on large household surveys and, since the same questionnaire was used in all the studies, it is possible to make comparisons between the cities.

In these studies, the UIS is defined to cover own-account workers and those working for small enterprises involving nine or less persons, with ILO criteria being used to classify such firms as UIS or UFS. Domestic servants were excluded from the UIS.

Some similarities emerge from the Peruvian studies concerning the characteristics of the UIS in comparison with the UFS:

1. While men form the majority of those working in both the UIS and UFS, they form a smaller percentage (and women a higher percentage) in the UIS than in the UFS.

2. Apart from there being a slight tendency for a higher percentage of the age group 14–24 years to be found in the UIS than the UFS, there seems to be very little age difference between the sectors.

3. Those in the UIS tend to have less education than those in the

UFS, where (with the exception of Iquitos) almost 50 per cent of those in that sector had some form of higher education, defined as all categories beyond Secondary education and including many technical and vocational courses.

4. Those in the UIS tend to earn less than those in the UFS, a characteristic that is particularly marked at the bottom end of the scale for those earning less than US$20 per month. The data bring out the heterogeneity of the UIS, as at the other end of the income scale there is a small percentage of those in the UIS earning over US$300 per month.

5. Almost all those working in the UIS tend to be either own-account workers or operating in firms involving no more than four persons, while the largest category for the UFS is that of large enterprises involving more than 100 persons.[8]

6. The percentages of the EAP in different economic activities was very stable across all the cities, with averages of 12 per cent in Final Goods Manufacturing, 3 per cent in Intermediate Goods Manufacturing, 5 per cent in Construction, 34 per cent in Commerce (including restaurants), 30 per cent in Non-personal Services and 6 per cent in Personal Services. The first three categories show considerable variations in the proportions of UIS and UFS workers involved, but the last three categories show very consistent patterns. Commerce and Personal Services are dominated by the UIS, with the majority of such workers operating as vendors. In Commerce one finds a large concentration of women UIS workers and this activity is characterised by low educational attainments and low incomes. In contrast, Non-personal Services, which includes professionals, office workers and public servants, tends to be a male preserve with an average of 70 per cent men across the cities in the sample. The level of education is much higher in this activity than in Commerce, though the level of monthly income is not uniformly higher – reflecting the fact that minor public servants are not highly paid in Peru. The relatively low percentages of workers in manufacturing reflects the high concentration of industrial production in the Peruvian capital, Lima.

---

8. Any reader who wishes to calculate the size of the UIS using the narrower definition of own-account workers only should multiply the figure for the UIS as a percentage of the EAP by the proportion of uni-person firms in the UIS.

Table 2.5 *Characteristics of the UIS and UFS for Seven Peruvian Cities, 1989*

City	Arequipa		Cuzco		Ica	
	Sector (%)		Sector (%)		Sector (%)	
Characteristic	UIS	UFS	UIS	UFS	UIS	UFS
Sex						
Female	47.5	30.6	48.2	31.0	39.3	33.2
Male	52.5	69.4	51.8	69.0	60.7	66.8
Age						
14–24	21.9	16.7	17.3	11.3	25.5	23.2
25–39	40.7	44.8	42.5	48.2	41.4	41.9
40–54	26.9	28.5	27.0	33.6	21.7	25.3
55 +	10.5	10.0	13.2	6.9	11.4	9.6
Education						
None	3.6	1.6	5.2	1.2	1.6	0.5
Primary	31.6	14.2	27.3	9.5	20.7	12.3
Secondary	46.3	32.9	52.5	35.5	53.1	40.9
Higher	18.5	51.3	15.0	53.8	24.6	46.3
Monthly income US$						
None	7.1	2.9	6.7	2.3	7.8	5.4
Less than 20	24.1	6.7	17.6	4.2	23.8	13.3
20–49	38.6	36.3	43.6	43.7	37.6	43.0
50–79	10.7	24.6	13.8	24.6	13.4	19.7
80–149	14.4	20.6	12.8	17.5	12.3	13.0
150–299	5.7	5.7	3.7	5.5	4.0	4.8
300 or more	0.9	2.0	1.0	1.3	1.0	0.8
No response	1.2	1.2	0.8	0.9	0.1	0.0
Employment by size of firm (persons)						
1	52.8	2.2	45.4	1.2	39.9	3.1
2–4	45.5	5.6	51.7	3.0	58.3	8.8
5–9	1.7	8.5	2.9	9.6	1.8	11.6
10–19	0.0	12.4	0.0	10.7	0.0	9.1
20–49	0.0	13.1	0.0	5.5	0.0	7.3
50–99	0.0	5.8	0.0	3.3	0.0	5.2
100 +	0.0	52.4	0.0	66.7	0.0	54.8
Economic activity						
Final goods [1]	51.0	49.0	78.6	21.4	55.3	44.7
Intermediate goods [1]	37.0	63.0	72.9	27.1	66.6	33.4
Construction	49.6	50.4	72.4	27.6	73.9	26.1
Commerce [2]	76.7	23.4	82.3	17.7	83.4	16.6
Non-personal services	8.3	91.7	9.8	90.2	12.7	87.3
Personal services	76.3	22.7	84.3	15.7	95.4	4.6

Notes: 1. manufacturing 2. including restaurants

City	Iquitos		Puno & Juliaca		Trujillo	
	Sector (%)		Sector (%)		Sector (%)	
Characteristic	UIS	UFS	UIS	UFS	UIS	UFS
Sex						
Female	44.3	28.3	49.9	29.3	42.0	34.4
Male	55.7	71.6	50.1	70.7	58.0	65.6
Age						
14–24	20.2	17.5	23.3	15.1	24.5	21.1
25–39	42.1	53.8	45.8	45.3	42.0	45.7
40–54	26.6	23.6	22.9	31.0	25.3	26.8
55 +	11.1	5.1	8.0	8.6	8.2	6.4
Education						
None	2.1	0.3	7.2	2.3	3.0	0.8
Primary	34.4	15.8	36.3	12.0	32.3	13.6
Secondary	52.8	47.7	42.1	33.0	48.0	37.6
Higher	10.7	36.2	14.4	52.7	16.7	48.0
Monthly income US$						
None	5.3	2.1	9.4	6.0	7.7	3.5
Less than 20	9.0	4.1	34.1	8.5	20.5	7.7
20–49	25.4	22.7	36.0	33.8	38.9	39.5
50–79	18.1	25.9	9.4	29.6	15.0	22.0
80–149	24.8	26.0	7.4	16.2	11.7	18.7
150–299	12.1	12.5	2.9	4.3	4.6	6.0
300 or more	2.7	4.4	0.3	1.1	1.0	1.8
No response	2.5	2.2	0.5	0.5	0.6	0.8
Employment by size of firm (persons)						
1	56.6	3.9	53.8	3.0	42.3	2.2
2–4	40.8	4.7	44.8	7.5	51.4	3.4
5–9	2.6	12.2	1.4	6.1	6.3	14.6
10–19	0.0	7.8	0.0	6.0	0.0	9.2
20–49	0.0	8.5	0.0	5.6	0.0	11.0
50–99	0.0	4.5	0.0	2.0	0.0	5.6
100 +	0.0	58.4	0.0	69.8	0.0	54.0
Economic activity						
Final goods [1]	80.8	19.2	92.7	7.3	73.8	26.2
Intermediate goods [1]	29.1	70.9	75.7	24.3	50.6	49.4
Construction	58.3	41.7	75.4	24.3	57.1	42.9
Commerce [2]	81.2	18.8	93.9	6.1	84.3	15.7
Non-personal services	12.1	87.9	14.7	85.3	16.7	83.3
Personal services	94.3	5.7	90.8	9.2	82.1	17.9

continued

Notes: 1. manufacturing 2. including restaurants

Table 2.5 *Characteristics of the UIS and UFS for Seven Peruvian Cities, 1989* continued

City	Arequipa		Cuzco		Ica	
	Sector (%)		Sector (%)		Sector (%)	
Characteristic	UIS	UFS	UIS	UFS	UIS	UFS
Hours worked per week						
Less than 35	26.4	15.8	21.3	17.3	33.5	24.8
35–48	30.6	61.5	29.5	61.0	27.7	48.8
More than 48	43.0	22.7	49.2	21.7	38.8	26.4
Total city population	596,673		208,445		153,920	
Total EAP in city	223,709		73,642		58,823	
UIS as % of EAP	36.8		47.1		46.4	

Source: IDESI (1991a–f), six studies, Tables 5 and 7 in each study. For a definition of the economic activities, see explanation in text.

7. While the modal group in the UFS works between 35 and 48 hours per week, the modal group in the UIS works more than 48 hours per week.

These Peruvian studies bring out very clearly the links between migration and informality. An unweighted average across the six studies found that 47.1 per cent of those working in the UIS were migrants, while for Domestic Servants, the percentage of migrants was 65.9 per cent. Iquitos is an outlier in the sample, since while the percentage of migrants in the UIS in the other cities ranges between 41.6 per cent and 62.9 per cent, for Iquitos it was 30.0 per cent. Similarly for Domestic Servants, the range of migrants for the other cities is between 62.2 per cent and 77.3 per cent; for Iquitos it was 30.9 per cent. If Iquitos is removed from the calculations, the unweighted average percentage of migrants in the UIS is 51.9 per cent and for Domestic Servants the percentage is 72.9 per cent.

The Chilean and Peruvian surveys were carried out in countries undergoing different macroeconomic experiences. By 1991, Chile had experienced a number of years of rapid growth in real aggregate income and this expansion in the output had created more employment opportunities in the UFS. In contrast, after a two-year boom encouraged by President García's stimulation of real wages, Peru was entering a period of economic crisis and falling output and wages that was to culminate in the economic chaos

City	Iquitos		Puno & Juliaca		Trujillo	
	Sector (%)		*Sector (%)*		*Sector (%)*	
Characteristic	UIS	UFS	UIS	UFS	UIS	UFS
Hours worked per week						
Less than 35	23.3	15.4	34.0	21.4	28.4	17.8
35–48	37.4	57.7	32.9	56.0	33.9	55.5
More than 48	39.4	26.9	33.1	22.6	37.7	26.7
Total city population	199,980		158,550		409,377	
Total EAP in city	69,929		58,173		154,166	
UIS as % of EAP	48.5		58.8		53.2	

and hyperinflation of 1990. However, despite the different economic situations of the countries and the use of slightly different definitions of the UIS, the results of the two surveys bring out some basic differences between the UIS and the UFS. They show that workers in the UIS tend to have less education and work longer hours than those working in the UFS (see also PREALC 1986, 1990b). There are also important gender differences within the UIS and these will be explored in more detail in the next chapter.

2.5 *Links between the UIS and the UFS*

Having presented data on the size of the UIS in Latin America and examined some of the basic characteristics of the UIS in two South American countries, it is time to return to the question of the relationship between the UIS and the UFS that was discussed in Section 2.2 above.

Here we shall consider two questions. First, what is the nature of the links (if any) between the UIS and the UFS? Secondly, if links exist, do they suggest that the UFS exploits the UIS, as is suggested in some analyses – such as the PCP approach or is the link a benign relationship that benefits the UIS? What of the further possibility that the link between the sectors may be symbiotic, in the sense that both may benefit?

The form of linkages

To examine potential linkages between the UIS and the UFS, one may first distinguish between socio/political links and economic linkages. Economic linkages involve direct transactions between own-account workers or small enterprises and those in the UFS, whether it be enterprises in the private sector or those operating in the public sector. Socio/political linkages are more tenuous, indirect and may be institutional in nature, such as when vested interests in the UFS are able to influence governmental action concerning the UIS. For example, arguments of 'unfair competition', 'health hazards' and 'congestion of public spaces' have been used by associations of UFS shopkeepers and traders to persuade governments to take legal action against some groups working in the UIS; see Box 2.2 for an account of the harassment of hawkers on the streets of Santiago.

Here we shall concentrate on direct, economic links. In considering direct links, one may distinguish between *backward* and *forward* linkages. Backward linkages are concerned with whether those working in the UIS obtain raw materials or other supplies from the UFS. Forward linkages exist when the UIS sells its output of goods and services to the UFS.

Backward linkages

That backward linkages exist is obvious from the casual observation of street sellers offering sweets, cigarettes and other branded products for sale. Clearly these goods have been obtained from the UFS, either from wholesalers or, more probably given the small scale of the purchases of UIS vendors, from retailers. Even where the vendors are selling goods that they or members of their families have produced – such as items of cooked food – some of the raw materials will most probably have been purchased from the UFS.

Other activities in the UIS, such as manufacturing or construction, are also likely to rely on the UFS to supply raw materials and other inputs to the process. Indeed, with the exception of pure service activities that require no other inputs, all other UIS activities will probably have backward linkages to the UFS either directly or indirectly, if inputs are purchased within the UIS from producers who obtain their raw materials from the UFS.

Forward linkages

Output from the UIS may take the form of intermediate goods, which are intended to be inputs into a productive process, or final

56

Box 2.2 The Hazards of Street Trading in Santiago (Chile)

Life is hard on the streets of Santiago for hawkers (ambulatory street sellers). Two surveys, each involving over 600 respondents, were carried out in January 1987 and January 1988, with the former also producing in-depth interviews with twenty respondents. The characteristics of sample members, which did not vary much between the two surveys, were that about 60% were men, three-quarters of the respondents were heads of households and about 60% provided the only income for the family. About 75% of the respondents had worked in another occupation before becoming a hawker and, within this group, about 45% had previously worked in the UFS, many taking up the new activity after losing UFS jobs, rather than by choice.

The surveys found that the vast majority (96% in 1987 and 87% in 1988) were trading without a permit, but this did not reflect a lack of interest in obtaining a permit on the part of the hawkers and a desire for illegality. On the contrary, one of the themes that emerged in the in-depth interviews was the willingness of the interviewees to pay for a permit and their frustration at having applied to the municipal authorities on many occasions without success.

Hawkers were and are the subject of much hostility from shopkeepers and others selling from fixed sites, accused at the very least of casting an unaesthetic blight on the city and more seriously of blocking pavements, of being a health risk through selling food without due regard to hygiene, of being unfair competition to honest shop-keepers through non-payment of taxes and other contributions, and of offering a cover for delinquents, such as pickpockets, who may take advantage of the crowded spaces created by hawkers. Using the lobbying powers of the organisations that represent them, shop-keepers put pressure on municipal authorities to limit the activities of hawkers, with the result that it is very difficult to get a permit. For example, in some parts of Santiago, permits are only issued to the disabled and only in small numbers even in these cases.

Operating without a permit meant that the hawker had continually to be alert in order to avoid detection and apprehension by the authorities, particularly the Chilean police (*los carabineros*). Most of those interviewed in the two surveys regarded this harassment as the worst aspect of hawking, since if caught the hawker almost always had his or her stock confiscated without compensation and, in many cases, would also be subject to fines or periods of between eight hours and five days under arrest or in gaol.

The confiscation of stock was particularly hard, as hawkers often had to invest most of their savings in their stock in order to have enough goods to sell to generate an adequate income. Confiscation made it difficult for a hawker to build up capital and increase the scale of the business, for example, by selling more expensive items that produced a higher profit. The result for many hawkers was that having lost their savings through the confiscation of their stock, they had to start again at the bottom of the scale and try to rebuild their business. (See PREALC, 1988 and Contreras and Thomas, 1993.)

goods and services, which are finished and ready to be sold to the consumer.

The output of intermediate goods may be linked to the UFS through sub-contracting, whereby small firms or own-account workers in the UIS make components or parts to be used by firms in the UFS. Even without contracts, small enterprises or own-account workers in the UIS may specialise in activities linked to supplying mainly the UFS, such as the case of scavengers who collect and recycle industrial and consumer waste products – see Birkbeck (1978, 1979) for a graphic account of the operation of workers on a garbage dump in Cali, Colombia.

The range of forward linkages for final goods and services is very wide, since while this output may be sold directly to the final consumer, it may also be demanded by firms in the UFS as an intermediate input into either production or distribution. An example would be an individual woman working at home with a sewing machine to produce sub-contracted items of clothing that are then labelled with a formal sector brand and sold in shops in the UFS.[9]

There are a number of benefits that enterprises in the UFS may gain by sub-contracting work to the UIS. First, an employer in the UFS may avoid having to pay the legal minimum wage or, possibly, having to grant wages that are above the minimum wage as a result of strong trade union pressure, since the wages paid by the sub-contracting unit in the UIS are not the responsibility or concern of the UFS firm. Secondly, the UFS employer is not responsible for whether or not social security contributions and other fringe benefits are paid to the workers by employers in the UIS. Finally, the UFS employer is able to adjust output to fluctuations in demand by varying the amount of sub-contracting undertaken, rather than through varying the size of his or her own labour force. The latter might involve costs of adjustment, such as the need to make redundancy payments when sacking workers during a recession and the costs of finding and possibly having to train workers when demand expands. These may be avoided by allowing the sub-contractor to bear the costs of adjustment.

If the goods and services produced by the UIS are sold directly to the final consumer, the forward linkage from the UIS to the

---

9. Homeworking such as this is not confined to the UIS in Latin America, as many women work this way in the UK and the USA. See, for example Hakim (1992) on the UK and Fernández-Kelly and García (1989) on the USA.

UFS is less clear. One possible distinction that could be made is whether the final consumer works in the UFS or the UIS, since it might be argued that if the consumer works in the UFS, purchases from the UIS represent a form of subsidy from this sector to the UFS. This argument has been put forward by some analysts of the UIS. For example, writing shortly after the publication of the ILO's Kenya Report, King (1974) discussed the UIS as a cheap-labour, low-cost-of-living subsidy to foreign firms based in Kenya:

> There are several elements in this, the chief of which is that the informal system, with its ingenuity, extreme hard work and massive competition, produces goods and offers services which have the effect of keeping the cost of living down, and thus allows large firms to continue to pay rather low wages to their workers. In particular, people who are employed in the lower end of the formal system (i.e., the majority) can live within these wages (i) because they have land and a wife's labour on it to supplement them and (ii) because many of their consumption, housing and transport demands can be met informally. Thus low wages and high profits in the modern sector are made possible by the much lower wages and tiny profits in the informal arena. (pp. 26–7)

In principle it would be possible to test the proposition that the UIS is encouraged by the UFS because it subsidises the wages of workers in the UFS by examining the extent to which the goods and services produced by the UIS are bought by those working in the UFS. In practice this has not been attempted and it would be difficult to design such a study. The first stage would involve a detailed analysis of the current expenditure patterns of UFS workers, in order to identify the quantities of goods and services they purchase from the UIS. This stage would be an important piece of research in its own right, as very little information in this area exists. The real problems come at the second stage, when the researcher would have to speculate on what the corresponding expenditure would have been in the absence of the UIS. The simplest answer would be obtained by substituting the prices of similar goods and services produced by the UFS, but this would be an overestimate of the subsidy as it does not allow for the possibility that the UFS might find it more profitable to fill the vacuum by producing cheaper goods rather than increasing UFS wages.

59

Competition between the UIS and the UFS

The discussion of sub-contracting above illustrates that co-operative links exist between those working in the UIS and enterprises in the UFS. What about competition between the sectors? Does it exist and, if so, how does the UIS survive? To answer these questions, we need to consider two areas in which competition might take place, first in the demand for raw materials and inputs of labour and capital (that is, in factor markets) and secondly in competition for sales of the output of the enterprise (that is, product market competition).

Factor market competition

Competition for raw materials may arise in activities such as manufacturing and construction and it is possible that expansion in the level of UFS output may lead to increased demand for some inputs that raises the prices to levels beyond the reach of those working in the UIS. To survive in such cases, UIS enterprises may need to find substitute raw materials that are not demanded by the UFS. For example, in response to sharp increases in the price of leather, some shoe-makers in the UIS have switched to using rubber from old tyres to make the soles of cheap sandals.

There may be competition for labour if some workers obtain basic training in the UIS and then find work in the UFS. The seriousness of the competition depends on whether the skills acquired through the training are firm-specific or general. If they are specific to the firm supplying the training, other enterprises will have little interest in hiring such workers. This is not the case for general skills and other enterprises may try to poach such workers away from the firm providing the training. As Velenchik (1993) shows in a study of apprentices and trainee workers in Africa, employers may reduce the costs of such poaching through contracts or by charging the worker for the training, often by paying the worker very little during the period of training.

Conversely, there is evidence of workers in the UFS acquiring skills and building up savings in order to leave the UFS and enter the UIS either to become own-account workers or to start up small firms; see the discussion of Brazilian UIS weaving firms below.

Given the differences in the size of UIS and UFS enterprises and the differences in the technologies and capital intensities of the two sectors, there is little direct competition for capital inputs. Entrepreneurs in the UIS are limited in their ability to invest in plant and equipment by their lack of access to commercial banks and other financial institutions to obtain credit, so that usually they have to build up their savings – sometimes through wage employment in the UFS. For example, Reichmuth (1978) reports that in a study of the clothing sector in Lima, 71 per cent of UIS enterprises were started with the owner's savings and that about half had been earned elsewhere, generally in the UFS.

Lack of credit tends to make entrepreneurs in the UIS reliant on second-hand capital equipment, often obtained in the form of obsolescent plant and tools discarded by the UFS. This method of capital accumulation enables enterprises in the UIS to survive, but does not allow much scope for changing the technology of production. The problem of credit will be discussed in more detail in the next chapter.

Product market competition
This will depend on a number of factors concerning the type of good or service being provided and the location of the enterprise.

1. Firms in the UIS may offer cheaper alternatives to the goods available from the UFS and therefore be able to compete in terms of price. The example given above of UIS shoe-makers selling sandals based on recycled rubber tyres is an example of this kind.

2. The UIS enterprise may be able to find a niche within which it can operate without being threatened if it can offer something that UFS enterprises would find it difficult to offer on a competitive basis. These niches sometimes depend on the location of the enterprise. For example, there may be little competition when the UIS enterprise is producing a good that is consumed by those working in the UIS and is situated in a location frequented by these workers, or is convenient for workers in the UFS. For example, cooked food produced and sold from the homes of people living in poor *barrios* may compete for customers with alternative UFS sources of meals. An example is given in Box 2.3 below, while an interesting study of linkages between the UIS and the UFS and the need to find niches in an unusual situation is the study of Salvadorean refugees in Costa Rica in Basok (1993).

Benign, exploitative or symbiotic links?
The question of whether the links between the UIS and the UFS exploit the UIS have a benign effect or are symbiotic is an impor-

Box 2.3 Finding a Niche as a UIS Enterprise

Retailing in Santiago. Tokman (1978b) presents an interesting case study of the competition between small shops and supermarkets for sales of food, commenting on the fact that one Chilean supermarket chain had closed all its branches in low income areas of Santiago after more than ten years of unsuccessful competition with small shops.

Data are presented to show that small shops charged higher prices for comparable items than supermarkets. The size of the differential increased with the distance of the shop from the supermarket, but still averaged about 9% even when the shop was within 100 metres of the supermarket. The explanation proposed for the survival of the small shop and its ability to charge higher prices than the supermarket was that there were imperfections in both product and factor markets.

In the product market, the small shop was able to cater to the need of poor customers to shop frequently for small quantities - a 1974 survey in Santiago found that whereas 42% of high income households shopped weekly, 47% of low income households shopped daily. Thus, while it would make no economic sense for a supermarket to sell individual eggs or cigarettes, since it relies on the rapid turnover of large quantities of goods that are prepacked in standard units, the small shop was willing to sell in this way. In addition, poor customers were often able to obtain credit in small shops (about 50% of the small shops in the survey provided credit to customers).

In factor markets, the small shops are at a disadvantage with respect to the supermarkets in terms of the prices they have to pay for their supplies. Whereas the supermarkets possess considerable bargaining power through bulk purchasing, small shops have problems in purchasing cheaply; in addition to the problem of the size, they also lack access to the credit that would allow them to buy larger quantities and hold inventories. Indeed the survey found that in about 10% of cases, small shops actually bought their supplies from supermarkets or other retailers. Data collected in the survey suggest that even though the prices charged by small shops are higher, the mark-up obtained may be lower than that gained by the supermarket.

The way in which the small shops survive and the reason they continue is that typically they provide work for unpaid family workers (including children), work longer hours per day and are open more days per week than the supermarket. The small shop also relies on proportionately less capital than the supermarket; 82% of owners lived in the building where the shop operated and in many small shops the only capital was a pair of scales, though some would also have a refrigerator. Tokman shows that when the provision of work for family members and the implicit rate of return on capital is taken into account, the small shop was operating efficiently and this enabled it to compete with the supermarket.

tant one, but not easy to answer until we have a more precise idea of what is meant by 'exploit' and 'benign', since both words have emotive connotations. The Marxian approach provides a clear description of exploitation in terms of the extraction of surplus value.[10]

Desai (1979) describes a Marxian model:

> [that] divides the economy into three sectors, the monopoly sector, the competitive sector and the state sector. The monopoly sector is technologically progressive, with high wages and high relative rates of surplus value where trade unions play an active role in bargaining and where cost plus pricing is the rule. The technologically progressive nature of the monopoly sector means that even in expansionary phases, it expands its employment by small amounts. On average, it sheds labour instead of absorbing it. This labour, along with many less skilled and underprivileged workers (women, immigrants, blacks, youth) form the labour force in the competitive sector. Here the technology is not very progressive and absolute amounts rate of surplus value is the source of profit. Output expands by expanding employment. In this sector unions have to struggle for recognition. It includes the reserve army of un-employed – those who are 'hired last and fired first' ...
>
> The monopoly sector needs the competitive sector as a supplier of reserve labour as well as of raw material and component inputs. The pricing system transfers surplus value from the competitive sector to the monopoly sector. (pp. 208–9)

With only minor changes, one might interpret the monopoly and competitive sectors as the UFS and UIS respectively and, if one accepts a Marxian analysis, the question of exploitation would seem to be settled affirmatively. Not only are entrepreneurs in the UFS extracting surplus value from workers in that sector, they are also extracting surplus value from the UIS as a whole and leaving very little for entrepreneurs in the UIS, as the reference to 'tiny profits' in the earlier quotation from King suggests.

However, while a Marxian approach is widely used by sociologists and political analysts, it does not represent the dominant

---

10. In this analysis, capital extracts surplus value from labour by being able to set the exchange-value of labour lower than the use-value of labour. In non-Marxian terminology surplus value would approximate value added minus the wage-cost of labour. See Desai (1979) for a full technical discussion of Marxian terminology.

mode of analysis among economists, for whom 'exploitation' lies outside the framework of economic analysis. The orthodox neo-classical economic explanation would be based on a model in which it is assumed that those in the UIS are trying to maximise their satisfaction subject to the constraints under which they have to make choices. The constraints for those working in the UIS are likely to be severe, including lack of education and skills, lack of access to credit and capital, and, possibly, market distortions that prevent them entering the UFS. However, given the constraints, the model assumes that if they choose to sell to the UFS, then this must represent the best alternative available to them and that any other strategy would make them no better off (otherwise they would have chosen it).

To the extent that there are market distortions, such as the government favouring the UFS through subsidised credit or tariffs to protect its domestic market, the neo-classical model would predict that those working in the UIS would be better off if the distortions were removed. This is the basis for arguments put forward by organisations such as the World Bank that in the long run the freer operation of market forces will benefit the poor.

The Marxian and neo-classical views of exploitation represent opposite ends of the theoretical spectrum and the differences in their assumptions and mode of analysis make it difficult to see how an appeal to empirical evidence can settle the question between them. However, even if one cannot appeal to empirical evidence to resolve the theoretical question, it is possible that detailed studies of the UIS may shed light on the conditions under which links with the UFS take place.

Two studies addressing this issue and relating to Latin America are Reichmuth (1978), which studied the clothing industry in Lima, and Schmitz (1982), which examined parts of the textile industry in Brazil. Detailed summaries of both studies are presented in Harriss (1990).

Reichmuth found that the UIS clothing industry had strong backward linkages to the UFS for raw materials and he suggests that the higher prices paid by UIS firms (as compared with firms in the UFS) may reflect the high fixed costs involved in small scale transactions. There were also strong forward linkages to the UFS through sub-contracting. In the case of some UIS firms, there was a direct dependency on firms in the UFS for working capital. Market relationships between UFS and UIS producers were both complementary and competitive:

The Urban Informal Sector

- there was very little UIS participation in the high-income clothing market, but
- UIS producers supplied a considerable share of the middle-income market, either through sub-contracting to UFS firms (complementarity) or direct personal contacts with clients, and
- UIS producers were the main suppliers to the low-income clothing market.

One interesting feature of Reichmuth's study was that it examined how linkages varied over time. His results suggest that the degree of complementarity increased when demand was expanding and that there was more competition between the UFS and the UIS when demand declined.

Schmitz (1982) studied branches of the textile industry in three Brazilian towns (knitting and clothing in Petrópolis, hammock-making in Fortaleza and weaving in Americana). As in the Lima study, there were strong backward linkages to the UFS in all three branches. One feature was that because of their informal nature and lack of registration, most UIS producers were unable to buy raw materials directly and had to make purchases through intermediaries, which meant that in the case of the knitting industry they paid 25 to 30 per cent more than medium or large firms. UIS hammock makers, for example, often had to buy their cotton from UFS hammock manufacturers.

Forward linkages varied. The knitting industry mainly supplied shops, many of which were sales outlets for UFS firms in the industry. They were able to compete with output from the UFS because of their flexibility to change design to order:

'We, who work on a small scale, can manage all types of hooks and eyes, loops and fancy stitching.' This flexibility in responding to small orders of different types is one of the most important factors in the survival and growth of these producers. (Schmitz, p. 75)

The degree of involvement of the sample of UIS hammock-makers in sub-contracting varied and was sometimes undertaken when they were unable to obtain raw materials, but in general they sold to the local market through small shops and market stall holders.

A majority of those in the sample of UIS weaving firms had been employees in UFS firms and had become independent in order to 'improve their economic and, thus, social situation' (p. 136). The

65

majority were sub-contractors attached to a parent firm in the UFS but, given the degree of competition among sub-contractors, 'they find themselves unable to negotiate the piece rates, having little choice but to accept the parent firm's terms' (p. 137).

Discussing the linkages from a Marxian viewpoint, Schmitz considered the experiences of sub-contractors versus independent producers in the UIS:

> In order to give at least an indication of the extent to which the surplus can or cannot be retained by a small subcontractor, his earnings can be compared with those of an independent producer (provided they work under otherwise equal conditions). In the case of the hammock industry we were able to make such a comparison which showed that the independent producer earned roughly twice as much as the subcontracted producer. This would suggest that the surplus syphoned off was indeed substantial. (p. 171)

Schmitz suggests that an even bigger problem than this degree of exploitation is the irregularity and uncertainty of work and payment for those involved in sub-contracting and this is clearly an area where firms in the UIS are in a weak position in relation to the firms they are linked with in the UFS.

This is a study of considerable interest, but the reader should note that the results are based on a detailed analysis of a small number of UIS enterprises. For knitting, the sample included eight UFS firms and five UIS firms; for hammock-making the sample was eight UFS and eight UIS firms and for weaving the sample was twenty firms, of whom twelve had fewer than ten workers.

While the two studies reported here provide some information on the relationship between the UIS and UFS in a manufacturing activity, there is still much research to be done in order to increase our knowledge of other activities (in commerce and services, as well as in manufacturing) and other countries.[11] However, on the basis of the studies reported here, one would expect access to raw materials to be a major problem for UIS firms and sub-contracting to be important in many branches of manufacturing.

---

11. Fields, Chan and Gindling Jr. (1985) carried out a survey of 30 informal and small formal enterprises in San José (Costa Rica) in 1985. The enterprises were in commerce, industry and repairs and the findings suggested that the linkages between the UIS and the UFS were more benign than they were in the studies cited above.

2.6 *Conclusions*

This chapter has attempted to lead the reader through the difficulties of defining the UIS and has discussed the problems of measuring its size. Statistical data have been presented to illustrate the importance of the UIS in Latin America over recent decades and the structure of the UIS in two countries, Chile and Peru, has been explored. The data for Peru showed a skewing of the income distribution in the UIS, with a higher proportion earning less than US$50 per month than was the case for those working in the UFS.

The main method by which the UIS can survive and either compete or co-operate with the UFS is by offering large quantities of labour-time at very low cost, a process that has been described as 'self-exploitation' (Singer 1992, p. 59). As the studies presented above demonstrate, workers in the UIS tend to work more hours per week than those in the UFS, which may involve working more days per week. For example, a study of hawkers in Santiago (Contreras and Thomas, 1993), found that 44 per cent worked six and 43 per cent seven days a week, compared with five or five-and-a-half days in the UFS. We have explored the question of whether this should be explained in terms of capitalist exploitation of the poor or the existence of a labour supply in excess of the demand for jobs in the UFS and suggested that it is difficult to provide a theoretical framework within which the concept of 'exploitation' can be both defined and tested.

However, there is substantial evidence that those working in the UIS are disadvantaged by lack of education and training, lack of access to credit and many other problems. We shall explore some of these difficulties, as well as the links between the UIS and poverty, in the next chapter. Finally, in Chapter 4, we shall consider the impact of the debt crisis and structural adjustment on the UIS in Latin America.

Surviving in the City

Appendix A Country List of Studies of the UIS in Latin America

Argentina   Sánchez et al. (1981).
Bolivia   Blanes (1989); McFarren (1992).
Brazil   Despres (1990); Jatobá (1989); Tosta Berkinck
                   (1981).
Central America   Haan (1985); Pérez Sáinz and Menjívar Larín
                   (1991, 1994).
Chile   Contreras and Thomas (1993, 1994);
                   MIDEPLAN (1992); Pollack and Uthoff
                   (1989); PREALC (1987c).
Colombia   Cartier and Castañeda (1990); Cortes, Berry
                   and Ishaq (1987); Forero Pardo (1991),
                   Lanzetta de Pardo et al. (1989); Mohan
                   (1986).
Costa Rica   Basok (1993); Fields, Chan and Grindling
                   (1985); Herrick and Hudson (1981); Pollack
                   (1989).
Dominican
Republic   Kleinekathoefer (1987); Murphy (1990).
Ecuador   Middleton (1991).
El Salvador   Basok (1993).
Guatemala   Arturo et al. (1989).
Mexico   Benería (1992); INEGI (1990); Murphy and
                   Rees (1990); Roberts (1989); Selby, Murphy
                   and Lorenzen (1990).
Nicaragua   Pérez-Alemán (1992).
Panama   Camazón, García-Huidobro and Morgado
                   (1989).
Peru   Carbonetto and Carazo (1986); Carbonetto,
                   Hoyle and Tueros (1987); de Soto (1989a);
                   IDESI (1991a–f); PREALC (1987b);
                   Strassmann (1986); Villarán (1993).
Uruguay   Fortuna and Prates (1989); Grosskoff and
                   Melgar (1990); Portes, Blitzer and Curtis
                   (1986).
Venezuela   Márquez and Portela (1991).

68

3 Social and Economic Problems Facing the Urban Informal Sector

3.1 *Introduction*

Chapter 2 provided an overview of the UIS, discussed its structure and explored the links between the UIS and the UFS. In this chapter we shall consider further characteristics of the UIS and a number of the problems faced by those working in that sector.

The earlier discussions of the role of the UIS in providing a means of survival in cities for those who are unable to find employment in the UFS have suggested that many of those in the UIS are poor. However, the heterogeneity of the UIS also suggested that not all those in the sector are poor and the income data presented in the previous chapter showed a considerable overlap in the income distributions of the UIS and of the UFS, with that of the former being skewed to the left towards lower incomes. Clearly, the link between the UIS and poverty is neither simple nor obvious and this relationship will be explored in Section 3.2.

While some of the tables in Chapter 2 present data on women in the UIS, the information was concerned with broad aggregates and did not bring out important gender differences between the sexes in their experience in the UIS, where women are often in a vulnerable position. The role of women in the UIS and the particular problems they face are discussed in Section 3.3, where more detailed information and case studies will be presented. Children represent another vulnerable group within the UIS and an account of their problems will be given in Section 3.4.

Readers living in Europe or the USA probably take for granted the fact that governments and other agencies in their respective countries supply a variety of social services, such as free education, free (or subsidised) health care, sickness and unemployment benefits, and pensions. The situation is rather different in Latin American countries, where very little social protection is available,

69

even in countries that (on paper at least) have comprehensive programmes. The state of social security in Latin America and its future prospects will be discussed in Section 3.5.

As was shown in Chapter 1, migration has played a very important role in the growth of the urban population in many Latin American cities. Migrants need homes. On arrival, being poor, many had to move into overcrowded slums or seek shelter by taking part in land invasions as part of the development of squatter settlements. Shanty towns, which feature prominently in most Latin American cities, and housing problems will be discussed in Section 3.6. Having surveyed these problems, conclusions are presented in Section 3.7.

3.2 *The Link between the UIS and Poverty*

The first issue that arises in examining the link between the UIS and poverty is the problem of how to define poverty. There has been considerable debate over whether poverty can and should be defined in absolute terms or is a relative concept (see Sen (1983, 1984) for example). For a technical discussion of the measurement of poverty and poverty indicators the reader should consult Boltvinik (1994), Fields (1994) and Streeten (1994).

In considering extreme poverty, where individuals or families are suffering from malnutrition and have inadequate housing, clothing or health provisions, one approach is to see whether the individual or family is able to meet the cost of the basket of goods and services that would satisfy this basic set of needs and, if not, the magnitude of the shortfall. While such a basic basket would vary among countries (for example, the need for heating fuel is less in a hot country than in a cold one), this approach gets close to the idea of absolute poverty. The cost of the basic basket of survival goods may be used to provide a poverty line to be used in the analysis of poverty. Those who are unable even to purchase the basic basket of goods and services required for survival are often labelled as being extremely poor, or destitute.

Those in relative poverty are able to meet the costs of the basic survival basket, but are still in the lower tail of the income distribution in a country. Here there may be problems of overcrowded housing, lack of adequate access to clean water, sanitation facilities and other resources which, while not being life-threatening, represent deprivation in relation to the rest of the population. This concept could be incorporated into the analysis of poverty in several ways. For example, the cost of overcoming the deprivation could be calculated and used to establish an upper poverty line for those who were not destitute, but still poor. Alternatively, individuals or families that were above the destitution poverty line, but suffered some deprivation (as represented by a checklist of facilities), may be classified as poor without measuring the exact degree of poverty.

While it is possible to construct the basic basket of goods and services for survival and compute its costs, establishing the basic poverty line may cause problems in practice. In empirical studies describing poverty in particular countries, the resources available may not be sufficient to carry out the calibration exercise. In such cases, the poverty line is defined in relation to some income or earnings figure that is easier to obtain. For example, in PREALC (1991a), average income is defined as three-quarters of the value of per capita GDP. Using this average income figure, an upper poverty line is defined as 33 per cent of average income, while the destitution poverty line is set at 17 per cent of average income.

Another base line that has been used in many studies is the statutory minimum wage or salary, with the poverty line being set as some fraction of this value. One problem with this approach is inflation; unless the government adjusts the nominal value of the statutory minimum wage in line with inflation, the real value falls. This happened in a number of Latin American countries that suffered from high rates of inflation, particularly when governments were carrying through structural adjustment programmes that did not favour trade unions and minimum wage legislation. Thus from a base value of 1980 = 100 per cent, by 1991 the value of the real minimum wage had fallen to 56 per cent in Argentina, 33 per cent in Ecuador, 39.5 per cent in Mexico and, the most extreme, 14.9 per cent in Peru. The problem is that any measure of poverty based on a minimum wage subject to such cuts in real terms will give a distorted impression of the level of poverty. The moral is that the reader needs to check very carefully to discover exactly how poverty is being defined, especially when comparisons are being made across countries.

The Chilean Ministry of Planning and Co-ordination's 1990 survey (MIDEPLAN, 1992), was carried out in a way that solved most of the problems outlined above; the basic basket of goods and services necessary for survival was constructed (concentrating particularly on adequate nutrition) and its costs computed for both urban and rural households and individuals. Data were also collected on deprivation. Given this information, the destitute were defined as those whose incomes (including pensions and transfers) were insufficient to purchase the basic basket, while the poor were defined as those having an income less than twice the cost of the basic basket.

For the country as a whole, the report shows that despite its success in holding down inflation and achieving high real rates of growth in national income, poverty is still a problem in Chile. Among the urban population, 13 per cent were destitute, 26 per cent were poor and 61 per cent were non-poor; the rural percentages were 18 per cent destitute, 25 per cent poor and 57 per cent non-poor. The only positive note here is that the percentages had fallen since the previous survey carried out in 1987 of the urban destitute (16 per cent) and the rural poor (33 per cent).

The data reported in that study enable us to examine the linkage between the UFS, the UIS and poverty. For those working in the UFS, 10 per cent were classified as destitute, 25 per cent as poor and 65 per cent as non-poor, while the percentages for the UIS were 20 per cent, 30 per cent and 50 per cent respectively. As we see, the relationship is not a complete overlap between poverty and the UIS; first, 50 per cent of those working in the UIS were classified as being non-poor, and, secondly, 35 per cent of those working in the UFS were classified as being destitute or poor.

A similarly complex picture emerges if one relates poverty to the size of the enterprise, as shown in Table 3.1.

Table 3.1 *The Relationship between Poverty and Size of the Enterprise, Chile (1990)*

Size of firm	Destitute (%)	Poor (%)	Non-poor (%)
< 5 persons	65.2	51.3	39.9
> 6 persons	34.8	48.7	60.1
Total	100.0	100.0	100.0

Source: MIDEPLAN (1992), p. 425, Annex Table 14.

The data show that while large percentages of the destitute and the poor are found in enterprises involving five or fewer workers (including the employer), there are also substantial percentages in firms involving six or more persons.

Having studied links between the UIS and poverty in Venezuela in 1987, Cartaya (1994) concluded:

In general, this study suggests that informality is strongly associated with the *intensity* of poverty. But this relationship appears only when informal workers are analyzed by industry sectors and type of employment (employer, worker, self-employed). Within the poorest households are concentrated the lowest paid informal and modern sector workers. The poorest households also are those whose characteristics increase their vulnerability to poverty, including characteristics of labor supply that, when matched to the demand for labor (segmentation of the labor market), leave them open to discrimination. Thus, the poorest households frequently are those with elderly workers, those headed by young women, those whose workers have low education levels, and those where children constitute an important proportion of all household members. (p. 243)

The conclusion to be drawn is that, at the aggregate level, both the UFS and the UIS straddle the poverty lines proposed in this study. Given the heterogeneity of both sectors, there is no simple relationship between working in the UIS and being poor or working in the UFS and escaping poverty. We shall return to the MIDEPLAN study and look at some of the data disaggregated by sex in the next section.[1]

3.3 *Gender and the UIS*

Many early studies of the UIS did not take account of the different characteristics of men and women in terms of their opportunities, responsibilities and the constraints on their time. The result was that generalisations suffered from a gender bias; often results related only to men, only to women or were some unspecified average of the two. As we shall see, gender differences need to be taken into account.

In the context of development, Elson (1991) defines gender as follows:

Gender relations are socially determined relations that differentiate male and female situations. People are born biologically female or male, but have to acquire a gender identity. Gender relations refer to the gender dimension of the social relations structuring the lives of individual men and women, such as the

---

1. For further readings, see Annis (1988) and Infante (1993).

gender division of labour and the gender division of access to and control over resources. (p. 1)

Studies of the urban labour force in Latin America have shown that in many countries, while men form a majority of those working in the UIS, a higher proportion of women work in the UIS than in the UFS, so that this sector represents the majority experience for working women. How does the experience of women compare with that of men in the UIS?

Before considering this question, in order to put the labour market experience of women in a broader context, we shall examine some information on the relative average incomes of men and women in five Latin American cities. Table 3.2 presents data on male/female income differentials across a range of UFS occupations (plus domestic service), based on 1985 household surveys. The statistics are constructed by relating incomes to the average (set at 100 per cent) for the entire population (male and female) across all occupations. Thus in Caracas, in comparison to this overall average of 100 per cent, men earn 116 per cent and women 70 per cent. In Panama, male professionals are the highest earners at 317 per cent, while female professionals, who are the highest earners among women, only earn 180 per cent. In

Table 3.2 *Index of Average Incomes of Labour Force by Sex and Occupation, 1985*

Occupation	Bogotá		Caracas	
	M	F	M	F
Professionals	313	193	240	154
Technicians, etc.	197	154	138	71
Managers, executives, public administrators	540	373	205	175
Secretaries and cashiers	105	85	77	70
Commercial employees	89	43	102	76
Independent business-persons	163	78	118	49
Skilled & semi-skilled workers	75	49	89	60
Unskilled workers	61	51	75	46
Domestic employees	58	54	48	40
Total	116	74	116	70

Source: IDB (1990), p. 219, Table 2b.

other words, female professionals earn, on average, 57 per cent of
the amount earned by their male counterparts.

It is clear that with a few exceptions, women earn considerably
less than do men in the same occupational category. However, these
are broad categories and it is possible to think of several explana-
tions for the income differentials. For example, they may be due to
discrimination (whereby women are paid less than men for doing
the same job), or segregation (whereby men and women are involved in different activities within these occupational categories).

Scott (1986), through an extended analysis of the labour market
in Lima, presents results to suggest that segregation is the most
important factor. Using data from a 1974 Ministry of Labour survey
she found evidence that activities were 'gendered' within occupational categories. Within each occupational category, there were a
larger number of activities that were male dominated than were
female dominated, and the male dominated activities tended to be
better paid.

For example, among Professionals, activities in which men represented between 90 per cent to 100 per cent of the group included
architects, engineers, agronomists, doctors, dentists, lawyers and
accountants, while between 69 per cent and 89 per cent of university academics were male. In contrast, between 50 per cent and 89

Panama		San José		São Paulo	
M	F	M	F	M	F
317	180	200	175	340	142
164	118	167	125	168	72
195	158	234	124	347	191
91	101	98	50	95	102
110	76	93	69	114	52
67	51	116	79	149	69
88	67	81	73	86	93
69	65	75	63	40	33
60	33	80	46	28	20
106	88	107	85	117	62

Key: M = Male F = Female Average income of the entire population = 100.

per cent of secondary school teachers were women, as were between 90 per cent and 100 per cent obstetricians. For Professionals, women's average monthly earnings were 65 per cent of those of
men, despite the fact that the average years of education for women
were 99 per cent of that for men.

Among Office Workers, between 90 per cent and 100 per cent
of inspectors, depot workers, expediters, sales representatives and
customs officials were men, while between 90 per cent and 100
per cent of secretaries and typists were women. Women's average
monthly incomes were 83 per cent of men's in this occupational
group and women's average years of education were 109 per cent
of that of men.

Having looked at various religious and cultural factors that
have tended to lead to a 'sex-labelling' of activities into 'men's
jobs' and 'women's jobs', Scott (1986, p. 356) concludes that:

> In summary, then, gender segregation is anticipated in all the
> different phases of occupational orientation, training and recruit-
> ment. The effect is to direct women towards 'female' jobs and to
> equip them specifically for those jobs. At the same time it creates
> a number of obstacles – economic, political and ideological – to
> their obtaining access to 'male' jobs. It is therefore mistaken to
> view gender segregation as the outcome of labour market pro-
> cesses which are assumed to be sex-neutral, in which men and
> women compete on an equal basis for the same jobs.

Segregation into 'female' branches of activity was observed by
Bromley (1978b) in a study of Colombian street traders in Cali:
'About two-thirds of the traders were male and one-third female.
Male traders tend to have larger scale operations and to deal in
non-food items, while female traders tend to have smaller scale
operations and to deal in food items' (p. 1162).

In a further investigation of the labour market in Lima, Scott
(1991) examined the UIS (defined as consisting of enterprises
employing four or fewer workers). She found evidence of gender
segregation even within the manual workforce, with men predomi-
nating in activities such as painting, metal working, bricklaying,
shoemaking, printing and glass working, while women were to be
found in street peddling, retail selling, laundering, garment working
and shop assisting. One characteristic of this division is that the
men's activities showed a greater range of skill levels than those of
the women which, with the exception of garment working, were
generally classified as unskilled. Men 'had access to occupations
that facilitated skill acquisition, accumulation of savings and move-

ment between formal and informal sectors; hence a stronger position in the labour market overall' (p. 124).

One variable that might explain the segregation is the level of education of men and women and these were different; on average women had 4.3 years of education as compared with 5.8 years for men.[2] However, a more detailed analysis suggested that vocational skills were more important in explaining levels of earnings than was formal education. These vocational skills were obtained through workplace training and apprenticeships, but women were largely excluded from such opportunities, with the exception of garment working.

Scott argues that cultural factors and especially the family played an important role in the process of gender segregation:

The family undoubtedly did play a role in differentiating women's availability for work because of their responsibilities for child care, and this would have limited the extent to which they could participate in the formal sector. However, as far as the informal sector was concerned, it played a part in excluding them from certain resources and activities which might have been compatible with their domestic responsibilities. It was also influential in defining the status of activities that were designated for men and women – that is, their skill, commercial roles, and so on – thereby affecting the actual structure of informal sector activities. This partly explains why female activities such as cooking were not conceived as skilled and why the trade of dressmaking, even though skilled, was not accorded as much status as its male equivalent, tailoring. The higher status of male artisanal trades relative to female was also an effect of the historical actions of urban guilds, which defended them via negotiations with the municipal authorities. This was, above all, a public sphere dominated by men, for the gender ideology of the urban middle classes as well as the peasantry and urban

---

2. At the other end of the educational spectrum, FONCODES (1994) quotes Peruvian census data for 1993 showing that in Lima, aggregate illiteracy was 4.1 per cent, but this represented a rate of 1.9 per cent for men and 6.2 per cent for women. Illiteracy rates were much higher in rural areas. For example, in the sixth poorest region, Ayacucho, where the terrorist movement *Sendero Luminoso* began its campaign in 1980, the aggregate illiteracy rate in 1993 was 32.7 per cent, being 18.0 per cent for men and 45.8 per cent for women. However, the high rate for women may be confounded by the fact that their first language may be Aymara or Quechua rather than Spanish.

working class excluded women from participation in formal
politics. (1991, p. 126)[3]

A further important element exists in the private sphere of the
family, where women and girls bear an unequal share of the burden of reproduction and housework. These responsibilities limit
the hours that women can work and their ability to travel to
work, with the result that their range of occupational choice is
further reduced. Elson (1992) observes that:

... so long as women carry the double burden of unpaid work
in the reproduction and maintenance of human resources as
well as paid work producing goods and services, then women
are unable to compete with men in the market on equal terms.
Legislation for equal pay and opportunities and diminution of
'traditional' barriers to women working outside the home cannot by themselves free women from domestic burdens and expectations. Access to markets has benefits for women, but
those benefits are always limited, even if markets are entirely
free from gender discrimination. Benefits are limited because
the reproduction and maintenance of human resources is struc-
tured by unequal gender relations and because the reproduction and maintenance of human resources cannot be directly
and immediately responsive to market signals, so long as
human beings are regarded as having an intrinsic and not
merely instrumental value. (p. 37)

These problems in the public and private spheres affect women in
all countries, but they have a particular impact on poor women in
developing countries. Benería (1992) reports survey results showing that the Mexican debt crisis put increasing time pressure on
women:

For poor families, this often meant buying daily supplies from
street vendors whose products tend to be of lower quality than
those in regular shops. The tightness of budgets and the difficulties of storing food – such as with cases of unrepaired refrig-
erators – also reinforced this tendency; in such cases only small

---

3. Pérez Sáinz and Menjívar Larín (1994) present further evidence for important gender effects on the UIS in the major cities of the six Central American countries.

quantities can be bought at a time, therefore making shopping a daily chore, with the corresponding intensification of time spent on this aspect of domestic work. (p. 95)

Domestic service
While in some early empirical work on the UIS, the domestic servant was included, the case was put (in Chapter 2) for treating this activity as a separate category. While accepting this argument, it is still necessary to examine domestic service as it represents a major route into the UIS for many women (see Bunster and Chaney, 1989). To give an example, consider the case of the Bolivian woman outlined in Box 3.1.

While Soledad may be regarded as more successful than many women who start work as domestic servants, her story highlights a number of characteristics of this group.

1. She was a migrant. As the Peruvian data presented in Chapter 2 showed, this is true of a very high proportion of domestic servants who are often country girls coming to the city for their first job.

2. Though not discussed in this case, it is quite likely that Soledad was more fluent in Aymara or Quechua than in Spanish when she came to La Paz, which would have limited her job opportunities to domestic service, or some illegal activity like prostitution, where language skills are not of major importance. Through contact with her 'madam' and 'sir' and possibly through attending classes, she would improve her Spanish and be in a better position to operate in the urban labour market in the future.

3. Soledad chose to leave her post as a domestic servant to get married, but many domestic servants are forced to leave as a result of becoming pregnant (Bunster and Chaney (1989) present detailed interviews with domestic servants in Lima on this point).

4. The absence of family planning tends to lead to frequent pregnancies and the absence of social security or health care may put families into a position of poverty from which they may escape through the passage of time, as the children grow up. Selby, Murphy and Lorenzen (1990) present data for Mexico showing that:

Surviving in the City

Box 3.1 From Domestic Servant to Street Trader in La Paz

Soledad Quispe is thirty. She has a stall where she sells textiles on
the Avenida Max Paredes in the centre of La Paz. Fourteen years
ago she came from Achacachi on Lake Titicaca to La Paz to work as
a servant girl (empleada). In the large house in Sopocachi her sleeping place was a mattress in the glorified cupboard which housed the
electricity meters, brooms, mops and buckets. For more than sixty
hours a week she was at the beck and call of the family, for which
she was very poorly paid. After a year she had had enough of the
spiteful outbursts of 'madam' and the pawing attentions of 'sir'. Her
next, similar job soon proved to be no different from the previous
one. She had by now become acquainted with Filemón, at that time
25 years old, who had just landed a job at the SAID textile factory.
On her eighteenth birthday Soledad gave in her notice and got
married. The young couple lived in a small rented room and soon
had two children. They were not exactly well off; through people she
knew Soledad got a job as a washerwoman but she didn't like the
work. When the third child was on the way they decided to move to
the plateau, to El Alto, where they had bought a small piece of land.
With the help of friends, Filemón had built a one-room house there
with adobe bricks. But what should have become a time of renewed
happiness instead began badly. Their new daughter was a source of
anxiety; she had been born prematurely, she was weak and very
often ill. There was no money for the hospital and she died before
her first birthday.

When her mother came to live with them, Soledad could start
doing a daily job again. Together with her neighbour, Ana Escobar,
she sold food they had prepared to the building workers in El Alto.
She stopped doing that because she often argued with Ana about
money. Then she took up smuggling small consignments of textiles,
buying them in Peru and selling them to a trader in the centre of La
Paz. Eventually she was making four bus trips a week. In spite of the
cost of bribing the customs and the steady fall in the selling-price (as
more people were engaged in smuggling), she managed to make a
fair sum of money and save some of it. This became all the more
vital when the government's austerity programme forced the SAID
factory to close its gates and Filemón lost his job.

Soledad's textile business was meanwhile going from strength to
strength. She was now in a position to buy things from the women
smugglers herself and three women in the neighbourhood were knitting jerseys and hats for her from alpaca wool. From now on she
devoted her energies entirely to her textile stall in the city centre.
Unfortunately, her relationship with Filemón deteriorated more and
more. Perhaps he could not bear depending on his wife for money;
he also began to drink. Finally she and her mother threw him out of
the house. He is now most likely in the Yungas, in one of the gold
prospectors' camps. She does not know exactly.

Source: Direct quotation from van Lindert and Verkoren (1994), p. 46.

dren do not occasion the kinds of expenses among ordinary families that they do in the middle and upper sectors. ... When the children are young, they cannot earn income. But by the time they become 12 years of age, they are able to get some paid work and are able to contribute not just to their own costs but also to the general costs of the household. (p. 107)

The help of an extended family (Soledad's mother) can release women to find some kind of work.

5. Soledad's first job, selling food, is an obvious extension of the household skills she has acquired as a domestic and as a mother.

6. Her second job as a smuggler is less typical of the range of jobs generally available in Latin America, but Bolivia has a reputation for that activity; the *Mercado Negro* in La Paz, which sells contraband items during the day and stolen goods in the evenings, is well known both to tourists and the authorities.

7. The ease of entry into such an activity is illustrated by the steady fall in the selling price as the number of smugglers rose. By moving from smuggling to trading, Soledad was able to benefit from this fall in the supply price of the smuggled goods.

8. Soledad and her mother threw Filemón out, but in other cases he might have left on his own accord, as the practice is common in Latin America. ['Desertion is the poor man's divorce in Mexico and thus it is quite frequent among the economically disadvantaged throughout the country' (Bridges, 1980, p. 320).] As we shall see below, female-headed households form a high proportion of the families of those who work in the UIS and this is seen by many observers to correlate very strongly with problems of poverty.

Female-headed households
The MIDEPLAN (1992) report discussed in the previous section provides data for the whole of Chile on poverty disaggregated by the sex of the head of household and size of household – the latter being divided into uniperson and multiperson households. From Table 3.3, it is clear that of the total of almost 3.2 million households in Chile, the multiperson, male headed unit is the norm (76.4 per cent). Among uniperson households, the percent-

norm (76.4 per cent). Among uniperson households, the percentages of Destitute and Poor are higher for female- than for maleheaded households. However, looking at the average age of the two groups, it is over 60 for all three poverty categories of women. This would suggest that a large proportion of these women are likely to be widows, divorced or abandoned.

Among multiperson households, the percentage of Destitute households is higher for female- (15.9 per cent) than for maleheaded households (11.1 per cent), while the percentages of Poor households is very similar for the two groups. Comparing ages,

Table 3.3 *The Relationship between Poverty and the Sex of the Head of Household, Chile, 1990*

	Unipersonal households				Multipersonal households			
	Male		Female		Male		Female	
Poverty	(abs)	%	(abs)	%	(abs)	%	(abs)	%
Destitute	5777	5.2	7982	7.2	272147	11.1	84117	15.9
Poor	6389	5.7	10702	9.7	592039	24.2	125521	23.7
Non-poor	99612	89.1	91850	83.1	1581741	64.7	319552	60.4
Total	111778	100.0	110534	100.0	2445927	100.0	529190	100.0
% H/holds	3.5		3.5		76.4		16.6	
Av. Age								
Destitute	46.5		63.2		40.9		46.0	
Poor	49.9		61.0		47.7		51.9	
Non-poor	51.0		62.0		47.5		56.9	
Dependent								
Destitute	—		—		5.39		6.47	
Poor	—		—		3.73		3.78	
Non-poor	—		—		2.50		2.40	

Source: MIDEPLAN (1992), p. 421, Annex Table 13-A.
Key: % H/holds = Number of households in category as percentage of total number of households.
Av. Age = Average age of head of household (years).
Dependent = Dependency ratio: number of persons in household divided by number of workers in the household.

Table 3.4 *The Relationship between Poverty and the Sex of the Head of Urban Households, Chile, 1990*

Urban Poverty/ Sector	Unipersonal households		Multipersonal households	
	Male	Female	Male	Female
Destitute	100	100	100	100
UFS	27.7	00.0	54.1	20.8
UIS	72.3	53.2	45.6	39.9
DS	00.0	46.8	00.0	39.3
Poor	100	100	100	100
UFS	8.7	00.0	66.9	32.6
UIS	91.3	80.0	32.3	26.1
DS	0.0	20.0	0.2	41.3
Non-poor	100	100	100	100
UFS	58.8	52.1	73.1	56.4
UIS	40.2	30.1	26.9	30.6
DS	1.0	17.8	0.0	13.0

Source: MIDEPLAN (1992), P. 422, Annex Table 13-A.
Key: DS = Domestic Service.

one sees that for all three poverty categories, on average women are older than men. The other information presented in the table relates to the Dependency Ratio (DR), which shows that: poverty relates positively to the number of dependents in the household; and that among the Destitute, female-headed households have a higher DR than male-headed households.

Table 3.4 concentrates on urban households and provides a poverty decomposition according to whether the head of the household works in the UFS, UIS or Domestic Service (DS). What is striking here is the large percentage of domestic servants among both types of female-headed households that are Destitute, as well as among female-headed multiperson households that are Poor.[4] The high percentage of Destitute and Poor male heads of multiperson households working in the UFS reinforces the

---

4. Information on Domestic Servants is particularly difficult to quantify as much of their income may come in the form of income in kind, i.e. free food, lodging and clothing, which may not be fully accounted for in sample surveys.

point made earlier that the UIS and poverty are not synonymous.

While the level of family income seems to provide a plausible basis for the discussion of household poverty, there are two links missing in the chain connecting household income and poverty. First, the data do not tell us how much of the income goes into household expenditure, as opposed to being spent by individuals. Secondly, we do not know the pattern of household expenditure. Studies that have examined these links suggest that it may be an oversimplification to assume that female-headed households must be worse off than male-headed households with higher incomes.

Chant (1985, 1991) reports the results of surveys carried out among Mexican families that looked at the intra-household distribution of income, expenditure and consumption. The first finding of interest here is that although male household heads may earn much more than female household heads, total household incomes may not differ by as much when the earnings of other household members are taken into account.

Using data on a sample of 190 households, the average age of male household heads was 32 years and the average household size was 6.2 people; for female-headed households the averages were 40 years and 5.4 people. One result of the age difference was that children in the male-headed household tended to be younger than those in the female-headed household.

Turning to income data, the average weekly contribution to total household income of a male household head (in 1983 pesos, where £1 = 225 pesos), was 2,853 pesos as compared with 1,927 pesos for a female household head. Given the earning ability of young children is limited and that they need to be looked after, the average contributions of the spouse (422 pesos) and children (356 pesos) to total household income in the male-headed household were relatively small.

In contrast, since children in the female-headed household tended to be older, their earning capacity was higher and the average contribution they made to total household income was 1,204 pesos. As a result the average total household incomes were 3,630 pesos for the male-headed households and 3,131 for female-headed households; in per capita terms, the averages were even closer with 587 pesos per capita for the male-headed households and 580 pesos per capita for the female-headed households.

Turning to the linkage between household income and household expenditure, interviews in the study showed that whereas male household heads tended to retain some proportion of their income for personal use (in some cases up to 50 per cent), most female household heads contributed all their earnings to household expenditure. Chant (1985, p. 642) reports that the 'unequal allocation of economic resources often means, for example, that women and children are underfed or undernourished ... or that women and children bear the brunt of poor housing' and describes this situation as one of 'secondary poverty'.

In summary, while female-headed households tend to have lower incomes than male-headed households, to link this factor to poverty one needs to have data on the level and composition of household expenditure to explore the distribution of resources within the household.

The moral of this discussion of women in the UIS is that one must take care when generalising about the UIS that the conclusions are not merely statements about men. It is clear that gender effects must be taken into account. In particular, reporting economic data, such as average earnings or hours worked, may be misleading unless disaggregated by sex. The UIS is heterogeneous not only with respect to range of activities, size of enterprise, etc., but also with respect to gender and age. (See also Anker and Hein, 1986; Berger and Buvinic, 1988; Brydon and Chant, 1989; Buvinic and Lycette, 1988; Chant, 1992; Hirata and Humphrey, 1991; López, Pollack and Villarreal, 1992; Nash and Safa, 1985; Nuss, 1989; Radcliffe, 1992; Scott, 1994 and UN, 1989.)

3.4 *Children and the UIS*

Given a background of poverty and the need to survive, it is not perhaps surprising that one should find children under ten years old as well as adults working in the UIS. The conditions under which children work in developing countries has been of particular concern to two international organisations concerned with protecting workers' conditions and preventing the exploitation of childen, which have produced a number of empirical studies: the ILO, see Bequele and Boyden (1988); and UNICEF, see Myers (1991). From these and other studies a picture emerges of considerable variety. Children are to be found working in production, commerce and services, often in situations that seem totally inappropriate for such young workers (see Box 3.2).

Boyden (1991) provides an analysis of child labour, based on a number of studies carried out in Lima (see also Scott, 1982). Obtaining accurate estimates of the scale of child labour from official sources is difficult, since the questions used in the census are only likely to pick up full-time child workers, rather than those attending school and working part-time or at weekends.

Box 3.2 Child Workers in Bogotá's Quarries and Brickyards

Bogotá has experienced very rapid population expansion, with annual growth rates of 7 per cent per annum during the 1960s and, in the absence of any building programmes of cheap housing, a large proportion of the population lives in the Eastern Zone, a series of squatter settlements built on the slopes of the Andes. Given the terrain, among the main occupations of the squatters are quarrying and brickmaking. Child labour is widespread in both these occupations. Information on conditions in these activities was collected through a survey of about 100 children and 26 adults in 1988.

Quarrying. Most of the children work in quarries run by small enterprises that operate without an official permit. These enterprises tend to operate with low levels of technology, using primitive techniques and obsolete machinery. They rely on manual labour, including child labour, working up to 12 hours per day, compared with the 8 hours per day for workers in the larger, registered quarries. Children usually work as assistants to their parents or other adults rather than being employed directly. After large rocks and aggregates are extracted, the latter are fed into hoppers which feed the crushers. From here the material passes through a process involving sieves of various sizes to separate out the different substances, such as sand and gravel. Children work both at shovelling material into the hoppers and at sieving. About half the children received payment in kind only and more than one-third of those who received cash said that their wage was paid to their parents. The daily cash wage for children in the quarries was (in 1988) less than one US$.

Brickmaking. Small brickmaking enterprises are family concerns and the families live on the site, so that the brickyard typically contains the family dwelling, a kiln and a primitive mill (turned by a mule or donkey) and pit for mixing the clay and kaolin with water. In addition to the children of the family, others are hired to help with the work. These enterprises were labour intensive and most of the bricks produced were sold to other low-income families to build their own houses in squatter settlements. Children were mainly involved in transporting and stacking bricks; piling up bricks after they have dried in the sun, loading them into the kiln for firing and stacking them afterwards and, finally, loading them onto trucks. They were also used to lead the mule or donkey driving the mill and to carry coal to the kiln. Men undertake the heavy task of excavating the clay from the mountainside and women mainly mould the bricks, though children may help in this work. About half the children surveyed worked five to seven days per week and about 20% worked 8 to 9 hours per day. The work involved some danger and many of the children had burns and bruises caused by the bricks. One 11-year-old boy had been so severely injured when a kiln exploded that both legs had to be amputated. Not being entitled to industrial compensation, his family had been paid about US$50 in damages by the brickyard owner.

continued

Many of the parents were illiterate and placed a low value on education. About 20% of the children had never been to school and only about 5% had gone beyond primary school. While many parents regarded work as a valuable way for the child to learn a trade, the unskilled, manual nature of the work makes this a dubious trade-off with formal schooling.

The recession in Colombia reduced the demand for bricks and made the activity increasingly less profitable, with rising costs for coal and transportation. Some brickmakers 'argued that they would probably close their brickyards if abolitionist laws on child labour were enforced and they were no longer able to hire children. The main reason for employing children is that they can be paid lower wages' (p. 59).

Source: Salazar (1988), pp. 49–60.

However, on the basis of ILO and other surveys, a reasonable estimate would be that about 10 per cent of children between the ages of 6 and 14 both attend school and work in the UIS during term time, with the percentage working rising to about 18 per cent during school holidays.

This study does not present a detailed quantitative breakdown of the distribution of child labour by occupation or activity, but a number of general themes emerge from the analysis.

Broadly, the children may be divided into *home-workers* and *away-workers*. The first group includes those who work at home, either as child minders (mainly but not exclusively girls) to release adults or older siblings for direct productive activities, or as part of a productive unit, such as daughters helping mothers in dressmaking or sons and daughters helping parents by cutting out leather shapes to make shoes or glueing wooden pieces to make toys. This work, which is generally unremunerated, is often undervalued by parents who underestimate the time children devote to these activities. Away-workers may be divided into those who work away from home in another house (or establishment) and those who work in the streets. There is some gendering among the former group, with girls frequently going into domestic service (one study found that 80 per cent of domestics were between 15 and 17 years old, with some as young as 8), while boys may be working for uncles or neighbours in a wide range of activities.

The range of activities undertaken by children in the UIS is very wide:

Some are involved in street services like shoe shining, washing cars or guarding property. Some work as fare collectors on buses. Others work in the market, cleaning fish, plucking chickens, carrying goods or selling leftover foodstuffs, or in restaurants, preparing food or washing dishes. Many are street vendors, selling newspapers, cheap household items and food. A few are shop assistants, apprentices in small mechanics or carpentry workshops, or cleaners in factories or restaurants.

The distribution of juvenile occupations corresponds closely with that of adults in the informal sector, although the greatest concentrations of children are in the lowest paid occupations, especially street vending and domestic service. There are no occupations exclusive to juveniles, except perhaps certain forms of entertainment on buses and in the street. Moreover, juveniles compete with adults in a range of occupations normally thought to be exclusive to adults, including hod carrying on building sites, washing up in restaurants and carrying goods in markets. Children are disadvantaged in relation to adults in that they are physically and mentally less suited to many jobs, but they have the advantage of being cheaper. (p. 34)

Street Children

It is important to distinguish here between children who work on the street, but who live with their family or in some other household, and those children who both work and live on the street. *Street children* are the most visible of child workers and have been the target of most attention from organisations concerned with the problem of child labour. There is a general realisation on the part of bodies, such as the ILO and UNICEF, that labour legislation banning child labour cannot realistically be enforced in situations of extreme poverty in which children either work or go hungry. As a result, the main objective has been to improve the conditions and future prospects of child workers. Boyden (1988) describes a number of programmes operating in Lima and elsewhere in Peru which have a number of common features. The provision of a midday meal for the children is a major contribution to improving nutrition, but to obtain it the children must agree to attend school or to take part in more vocational training schemes provided by the programme. In some instances the children are given extra food as a way of raising the living standard of their families. The children are encouraged to save and one programme (Manthoc) has made considerable progress in getting the children involved in organising and directing the programme.

Children who live on the streets have been the target of fear and suspicion in a number of countries. For example, in Brazil they are seen by the rich and the political right-wing as being:

> ... [a] blemish on the urban landscape and a reminder that all is not well in the country. Unwanted and considered human waste, these ubiquitous tattered, mainly black children and adolescents evoke strong and contradictory emotions of fear, aversion, pity and anger in those who view their neighbourhood streets, boulevards and squares as 'private places' under siege. (Scheper-Hughes and Hoffman, 1994, p. 23)

The result has been the operation of death squads that have routinely killed large numbers of street children, most noticeably in Brazil and Colombia.

This adds to the difficulties of those individuals and organisations trying to help street children, since not only are the children (and sometimes the members of the organisations) at risk from the death squads, but the organisations have to find the resources to provide shelter for the children as an alternative to living on the streets if they are to save some of those at risk.

The murder of street children has attracted the attention of many human rights organisations and it is to be hoped that their pressure on governments will eventually lead to a change of attitude and the enforcement of laws to prevent the death squads operating with impunity.

3.5 *Social Protection and the UIS*

Existing formal social programmes

While in some Latin American countries the armed forces and the civil servants were sufficiently powerful pressure groups to obtain pensions and other industrial benefits in the 80 years following independence, the main development of social programmes was based upon the system of social insurance that was developed by Chancellor Bismarck for Germany in the 1880s. This 'Bismarckian model':

1. provided separate programmes for different social risks (occupational, pensions, health care);

2. covered the employed, salaried labour force (especially urban workers);

3. involved contributions by the insured, the employer and the State;

4. and related benefits to contributions.

Mesa-Lago (1991) distinguishes between the statutory coverage (as laid down by law) and the statistical coverage, that reflects what happens in practice. He concludes that:

> under the statutory coverage, in most countries those insured are urban wage-earners and their closest dependents, whilst self-employed persons, agricultural workers, and those in domestic service, as well as the unemployed, and their dependents are not covered by social insurance; in addition, in a quarter of the Latin American countries (the least-developed ones) the coverage is limited to the capital and the larger cities. (p. 369)

> The Latin American countries with the highest degree of social insurance coverages are also those that have the lowest proportion of poor, but even in the most advanced countries the percentage of the population uncovered is greater than the percentage of those below the poverty line. (p. 373)

In other words, there is a strong urban bias and the poor are generally excluded.

In practice, even those covered by social insurance programmes have not done very well. In some cases benefits have not been indexed to the cost of living and inflation has greatly reduced their values. In other cases the programmes have been unable to meet their commitments through being in financial deficit, either because governments have raided the funds for other purposes or through high costs and inefficiency. Mesa-Lago (1991, p. 387) notes that in the mid-1980s administrative costs as a percentage of total expenditure, including benefits, were about 20 per cent in Bolivia and Mexico and 27 per cent in the Dominican Republic. In the latter country there were 20 civil servants administrating every 1,000 persons insured (as compared with 0.6 bureaucrats in Jamaica).

To these financial difficulties must be added the future effect of ageing populations with worsening ratios of beneficiaries to contributors. For example, in the mid-1980s in Uruguay the ratio of contributors to pensioners was already down to 1.25 (see also Lloyd-Sherlock, 1992). These problems have led many analysts to question whether the existing programmes can survive even with their current limited coverage, let alone be extended to cover the poor. One solution to the problems that is being advocated is privatisation and much interest is being focused on the Chilean experiment by a number of governments undergoing restructuring under neo-liberal policies (see Vittas and Iglesias, 1992 and Mesa-Lago, 1994).

Extending social protection to the UIS
Mesa-Lago (1992, p. 186) considers a number of problems in extending social insurance to the UIS:

1. Ineffective organisation and lack of political activity makes the UIS a poor pressure group in persuading the state to act.

2. The costs of financing social insurance coverage to the UIS is high.

3. The low incomes or no incomes (i.e. unpaid family workers) in the UIS makes obtaining contributions difficult.

4. The problems of detecting and inspecting the small units in the UIS makes collecting contributions difficult.

5. The current benefits to be obtained from existing schemes are unattractive, both in quantity and quality, for those in the UIS.[5]

Going beyond these general points, Mesa-Lago (1992) presents a detailed analysis of the possibilities of extending social insurance to cover the UIS in Costa Rica, Mexico and Peru and considers some of the alternatives. He comes to very different conclusions for the three countries.

For *Costa Rica*, where the UIS is relatively small, the social insurance programme (CCSS) has avoided problems of serious financial deficits and there has been little interest on the part of NGOs in providing alternatives to social insurance coverage for

---

5. For example, '[i]n Peru, groups of informal workers declared that they were not interested in becoming affiliated with social insurance because of the very low amount of the pensions, the poor quality of the health service, the time lost in waiting, and the long distances to services.' (Mesa-Lago, 1992, pp. 197–8.)

the poor, he concludes:

> The Costa Rican CCSS has the most solid system: its sick-ness–maternity program has a surplus and it is estimated that the pension program will achieve a balance in a few years (according to different calculations, some time between the early to mid-1990s). ... For the above reasons, social security appears to be the most effective channel for extending coverage in Costa Rica, subject to the reform of the pension program and a project to incorporate the self-employed that would reduce contributions and benefits. (pp. 198–9)

The picture is less optimistic for *Mexico*, which has a larger UIS and more problems with its social insurance programme. Thus:

> The Mexican Social Insurance Institute (IMSS) ... the institution legally responsible for extending social insurance coverage to the informal sector in Mexico, has suffered a persistent deficit in its sickness–maternity program and even though the pensions program has a surplus, it is showing a downward trend in income that will probably increase toward the end of the decade ... To summarize, despite the extension of social security coverage in Mexico (in particular, to the rural sector), there are serious doubts as to whether the IMSS is the appropriate instrument for extending coverage to the informal sector as a whole. On the other hand, there do not appear to be any suitable alternative methods. Only successful conclusion of an in-depth reform of the IMSS, together with a well-thought-out integration program, could provide the bases for commencing progressive extension. (pp. 200–1)

The most pessimistic picture emerged for *Peru*, which has the largest UIS and which suffered considerable economic dislocation under President García, but which has experienced a good deal of NGO activity and experimentation in programmes for the poor. Mesa-Lago concluded that:

> The financial situation of the Peruvian Social Security Institute (IPSS) is the most unsuitable for extension. The sickness-maternity program has a permanent deficit covered by transfers from the pension program, which has suffered gradual capital depletion. The latter has generally had a surplus, but this is decreasing in comparison to income and, in 1988, the two programs faced a serious crisis. ... There is a consensus that the

current social security model in Peru is not a viable channel for incorporating the informal sector and that only economic progress in this sector will allow it to be protected in the future, through either the market or the state or a combination of the two. In the meantime, the alternative methods appear to offer greater possibilities for protection and they should receive support from NGOs and international bodies. (pp. 201–2)

These three countries represent the spectrum of possibilities and it seems likely that among the other countries in Latin America there are more Mexicos and Perus than Costa Ricas. If existing social insurance programmes cannot be extended to cover the UIS, what are the alternatives?

Social protection for the urban poor

In the absence of formal social insurance programmes for the urban poor, governments have implemented various special programmes to avoid potential problems, since large numbers of destitute and poor people in the capital city, which is normally the seat of government, constitutes a political risk of riots and disorder (see Walton, 1987). One strategy has been to subsidise items that are important in the budget of the urban poor. For example, basic food items such as bread or rice have been subsidised, as well as fuel to keep down the cost of public transport. However, subsidies have been criticised by the World Bank and the IMF on the grounds that they are inefficient and distort prices. Governments obtaining aid from these organisations have been forced to discontinue them. The inefficiency results from the fact that not only the urban poor benefit from the subsidy, but also the rich who could afford to pay higher food prices. Distortions in the prices of agricultural products can have the effect of lowering the incomes received by local farmers and peasants, many of whom are as poor, if not poorer, than the urban poor.[6]

---

6. For example, analysing Peruvian data for 1985–86, Glewwe and de Tray (1989) found that although only 44 per cent of the population lived in rural areas, 70 per cent of the poorest 30 per cent and 83 per cent of the poorest 10 per cent of the population were found there. See Harriss and Moore (1984) for a more general discussion of 'urban bias' in development.

Targeting

After UNICEF had publicised the high social costs of structural adjustment (see Cornia, Jolly and Stewart, 1987), the World Bank softened its position somewhat over the problem of poverty (see, for example, World Bank, 1990b,c). While it still opposed general subsidies, it was less hostile to programmes that targeted the poor in ways that reduced the leakages of resources to those who did not need the subsidy.

Targeting is potentially more efficient than general subsidies in delivering aid to those in need and preventing it going to those who are not in need. However, in practice targeting can be difficult as it may not be easy to isolate those in need from the rest of the population when distributing aid. In some cases, the poor may be identified through *characteristic screening*, i.e. by using some characteristic that is particular to the poor. For example, it may be possible to target the poor by subsidising certain foodstuffs that are mainly grown and/or eaten by the poor. Another possibility is *locational screening*, i.e. if the poor live in particular locations, such as the slums or shanty towns in and around many cities in developing countries. Ribe *et al.* (1990) give subsidised rice in the Dominican Republic as an example of characteristic screening and the distribution of subsidised food through small shops in the *favelas* (shanty towns) in Brazil as an example of locational screening, since because 'better-off Brazilians prefer not to journey into *favelas*, even for the lower prices, the benefits go to those who need them' (p. 13). Other examples of locational screening are distributing free milk or school breakfasts through schools in poor areas, giving subsidised food to be used in community kitchens in shanty towns and providing basic medical care through health posts in slum areas.[7]

However, while targeting is more efficient than a general subsidy, it may not be as effective, in the sense that fewer of the poor may be reached through targeting than would have received the benefit under the general subsidy. Table 3.4 illustrates the trade-off between the two. A general subsidy should produce a zero Type I error (i.e. nobody being excluded from the programme), but possibly at the cost of a large Type II error, with many who do not need the subsidy receiving it. A perfectly targeted programme would only

---

7. An example of locational screening from nearer home is provided by the vans of the charities that dispense tea, soup and sandwiches to the homeless people sleeping in shop doorways on the Strand in London that I see regularly when leaving the London School of Economics in the evening.

deliver benefits to the poor, so that both types of error would be zero. An imperfectly targeted programme, the most likely case in practice, would probably produce both types of error. The problem for the policymaker then would be to choose what relative weights to attach to the two types of error.

Cornia and Stewart (1993) note that while the Type II error involves 'wasted' expenditure, the Type I error may involve a different type of cost. For example, poor children who suffer malnutrition through being excluded from a feeding programme may do less well at school and this may affect their earning capacity for the rest of their lives (see Pryer and Crook, 1988). The authors present comparisons of general subsidies versus targeted programmes using different weights to combine the two types of errors and also comparing the cost of the leakage (Type II error) with the welfare loss and the present value of foregone future income due to the failure to reach the poor. They conclude that 'the preliminary results arrived at in the paper suggest that "narrow targeting" may sometimes generate large welfare and efficiency costs' (p. 488).

Somewhat in contrast to these findings, a World Bank study that surveyed a large number of general subsidies and targeted programmes in Latin America (Grosh, 1994), concludes that targeted programmes have been much more progressive than have general subsidies, in terms of the quantity of benefits reaching the lowest quintile of the income distribution. Overall, the results suggest that care is necessary in choosing between subsidies and targeted programmes and it is important to examine each case on its merits.

Chile provides examples of subsidies and programmes targeting

Table 3.5 *The Trade-off between Efficiency and Effectiveness*

Result of programme	Groups in population	
	Poor	Non-poor
Group receives benefit	Target hit	Type II (inclusion error)
Group does not receive benefit	Type I (exclusion error)	Target hit

Source: Based on Cornia and Stewart (1993), p. 461, Table 1.

the very poor. During the dictatorship of General Pinochet, despite its appalling record on human rights, the authorities did carry out a number of programmes that were successful in reaching women (75 per cent in the PEM programme in 1986) and also had an equally good coverage of the rural poor as of the urban poor, which is rare in anti-poverty programmes (see Graham, 1993 for a detailed evaluation of the programmes). Alleviating poverty was one of the aims of the government of President Alwyn that succeeded General Pinochet and among the targets of their programmes were the young and female-headed households (see García, 1994). In many of these programmes, those to be targeted were identified through country-wide household surveys, such as the MIDEPLAN study discussed above. As the results showed, poverty reduction still has a long way to go in Chile. However, the possibilities for locational targeting should be explored in relation to anti-poverty programmes for those working in the UIS. (See also Folbre, 1993; Grosh, 1990; World Bank, 1990a, 1993b and Wurgaft, 1993.)

3.6 *Housing and the UIS*

Tables 1.1 and 1.2 in Chapter 1 illustrated the remarkable growth in urbanisation that has taken place in recent years. When the migrants arrived in the cities, they did not find large quantities of unoccupied housing waiting for them. Governments, both national and municipal, while generally doing little to discourage the migration, did even less to provide housing and the necessary infrastructure to support the urban expansion.

Before the explosion, the urban poor tended to be tenants living in tenements, such as the one in Santiago in 1941 described in Gilbert (1994, pp. 79–80) as having 18 rooms in which lived 140 persons, of whom 50 were children under the age of 15. While some migrants moved into such slum accommodation, the striking feature in many Latin American cities was the development of 'self-help' housing, that is poor people either bought or invaded land and built their own houses. Squatter settlements are not new in themselves and Norris (1990) traces them back in Brazil to at least the 1890s, but what was new was the scale of the process, as shown by the data in Table 3.6.

Gilbert (1994) suggests three reasons for this change. First, the development of mass transportation through buses made it easier for the poor to live farther away from the city centre, where land was cheaper or easier to invade. Secondly, in many cities the authorities either turned a blind eye or even encouraged poor

Table 3.6 *Growth of 'Self-help' Housing in Selected Latin American Cities, 1952–90*

City	Year	City Pop. ,000	Self-help Pop. ,000	%
Mexico City	1952	2372	330	14
	1966	3287	1500	46
	1970	7314	3438	47
	1976	11312	5656	50
	1990	11783	9470	60
Lima	1956	1397	112	8
	1961	1846	347	17
	1969	3003	805	24
	1981	4601	1150	25
	1991	4805	1778	37
Buenes Aires	1956	6054	109	2
	1970	8353	434	5
	1980	9766	957	10
Caracas	1961	1330	280	21
	1964	1590	556	35
	1971	2200	867	39
	1985	2742	1673	61

Source: Gilbert (1994), p. 82, Table 5.1.
Key: Self-help pop. = Percentage of city population living in 'Self-help' housing.

families to invade. Thirdly, increasing government budgets and improved technology made it easier to service the growing self-help areas of cities. Thus:

In Lima, Rio de Janeiro, Salvador, Caracas, Guayaquil and Barranquilla vast swathes of public land were occupied 'illegally' with the tacit approval of the authorities. Elsewhere, landowners were not punished for subdividing their land, despite the lack of services and planning permission. Of course, there were moments when governments attempted to stem the tide of self-help suburbia, but these were not common. The simple fact was that self-help housing represented a means by which the poor could be accommodated at little cost to the state. It was politically expedient to ignore the government's own planning regulations. The state not only tolerated self-help housing but encouraged its development through the gradual introduction of services and infrastructure. Water taps, electricity lines, schools and clinics slowly trickled into the self-help suburbs. (p. 83)

However, this passage does not imply 'that building a self-help home in a Latin American city costs nothing'. (Gilbert, 1990, p. 68). Not all governments encourage invasions and the majority of private landowners are positively hostile. As a result, land generally has to be purchased, often not cheaply and the price:

is often high when compared to typical wage levels and it will take several years to accumulate the necessary savings. As a result, subdividers sometimes sell on a loan basis, a 10 per cent deposit followed by the rest paid over a period of four years. (Gilbert (1990), p. 69)

There are also the costs of building materials and of obtaining water and sources of energy. Gilbert (1990) concludes:

There is no doubt that self-help housing does provide many of the poor with an adequate home. But it is only the less poor who can afford to buy the necessary land, materials and services; the really poor are often excluded from the self-help process. Such families are forced to rent rooms, or to share accommodation with kin. Given the severity of the 1980s recession, the fear must be that more and more people are being forced to live in rental and shared accommodation. Do-it-yourself works best when people have the money to pay for materials and services. (p. 70)

The high cost of land near city centres means that the poor often have to trade-off distance for lower prices or tolerance of invasion. Hardoy and Satterthwaite (1989, pp. 83–5) present a graphic account of a land invasion in Lima in 1971 that was initially opposed by the government. A week after the invasion, the squatters were offered and agreed to move to a large tract of land that was less commercially valuable than the site they had occupied, but was 20 kilometres from the centre of Lima (see also Lloyd, 1980). To the extent that bus routes were developed to service these new squatter settlements, and government, such as that in Peru, subsidised the price of petrol and hence the cost of urban travel, those in the UIS who had to travel to work were able to cope. However, when such subsidies were removed as part of structural adjustment programmes, travel costs became a major problem for many poor workers in the UIS. In addition, as Gilbert (1993, p. 125) reports from his research in Mexico and Venezuela, increased congestion added to the time spent travelling long distances by bus and cut into the potential working time of the poor.

Distance can also create other problems, since it may increase the difficulties (and costs) of obtaining services, such as water and sewage connections. Unless residents are careful, accumulated garbage and problems of sewage disposal can produce serious health threats, especially to young children (see Hardoy, Cairncross and Satterthwaite, 1990).

Attitudes to self-help housing
Attitudes have changed over time. Until the 1980s the reactions of governments tended to vary from tolerance *via* indifference to extreme hostility, the latter being particularly true of military dictatorships (see Perlman, 1976, on the slum clearances of the military in Brazil, and Benton, 1986, on Uruguay).

Early research by social scientists on squatters and slum dwellers was strongly affected by the pessimistic views of Oscar Lewis (1958, 1969), who saw them as being economically and politically 'marginalised' and living passively in a 'culture of poverty'. Other studies (Mangin, 1967, 1970 and Turner, 1967, 1968) saw a different picture and their analysis suggested that, far from being passive and marginalised, squatters who engaged in self-help housing were being rational in balancing their expenditure on housing against that on other necessities.

Turner's work has been very influential in producing a more positive view of the value of self-help housing in some of the international organisations, particularly the World Bank. The result has been international funding for programmes to help the poor help themselves by building their own homes. The programmes have been of two types; upgrading existing settlements, and site-and-services programmes.

Upgrading existing settlements
In the past, once an invasion had been accepted and the authorities were clearly not going to evict the invaders, the squatters would organise a leadership structure to improve the environment of the settlement and to begin the long and difficult process of persuading the authorities to provide services to the settlement (see Carlessi, 1989, and the other articles in that issue of the NACLA *Report on the Americas*). Getting electricity connected might be relatively simple, but water and sewage connections often took years. Using international funding from the World

Bank as loans, governments were encouraged to speed this process up. They negotiated programmes with the dwellers in self-help settlements whereby electricity, water and sewage connections were laid on now, to be paid for by the squatters over a period of years – see Salmen (1987) for an account of such programmes in La Paz. The scale of the problem is vast; FONCODES (1994) report that according to the 1993 Peruvian census, 29 per cent of all houses in Lima were without water connections, 32 per cent were without sewage services and 18 per cent were without electricity.

Site-and-services programmes
Rather than waiting for the invasion and then negotiating the provision of services, in site-and-service programmes, the authorities provide plots of land to the poor on which they may build their own homes, but these plots come with basic services already provided. In addition, the plot may contain part of the structure of the house, such as the main supports and the roof (and possibly a bathroom) when it is sold. In some of the more flexible schemes, where the authorities negotiate with potential buyers before building begins, the buyers may be able to choose the style or size of the house and also how much of it will be built before the purchase.

Between 1980 and 1987 the World Bank allocated about US$5 billion to urban projects, with most of this money going into upgrading and site-and-services programmes (Nientied and van der Linden, 1988). This programme was subjected to considerable scrutiny, both economic with respect to the efficiency of the programmes and ideological, concerning the effect programmes had on attitudes towards the poor (see Rondinelli and Cheema, 1988; van der Linden, 1986 and Ward, 1982).

One feature that was ignored in much of the debate was the issue of gender. As was shown in Section 3.3, female-headed households form an important group within the UIS and such families tend to be extremely poor. This, together with the precarious occupation of the woman and her low earning power, has meant that such families are often excluded from urban improvement programmes. Machado (1987) studied a number of such programmes in Brazil and concluded that:

> In designing housing programmes to reach [female-headed] households the following should be considered. First, women who are heads of households frequently take longer to build and/or complete housing because of other responsibilities for

their household: thus they prefer completed units to be offered. Second, because their income is lower than that of men who are heads of households they tend to have problems in securing and repaying loans and in meeting service charges. Third, the lack of infrastructure has more immediate consequences for women than men because of their reponsibilities for domestic work. Fourth, woman-headed households tend to have lower levels of access to essential services than do households headed by men. Thus if the intention is to help women, housing policies sensitive to gender roles and divisions are required. (p. 68)

Housing and the UIS

To survive in the city, the poor need work and somewhere to live. We have seen that for many the UIS solves the first problem and self-help housing the second. However, not all those working in the UIS live in slums or self-help housing and, conversely, not all squatters work in the UIS. There is a very large overlap between the two and the dynamics of the relationship may change over time.

For example, at the time of an invasion the male head of one of the families involved may be working in the UIS. If he later obtains a job in the UFS, it may not be sufficiently well paid for the family to be able to move. Conversely, a family whose head works in the UFS but which has limited savings may be able to obtain the biggest improvement in its housing position by squatting. Lloyd (1980) and Lomnitz (1988) present data showing the large overlap between squatting and working in the UIS for Lima and Mexico City respectively. Given this overlap, programmes to help the poor with their housing problems will, in many cases, be providing help to those who work in the UIS.

Urban improvement programmes are likely to continue, but with a greater emphasis on market forces. This is not a development that is seen positively by all analysts:

Nevertheless, serious doubts surround the current conventional wisdom on housing which relies so heavily on market forces. ... It is argued that the private sector, whether in the formal or the informal sector, can improve housing better than the state. Not only does this mean that government should generally leave construction to the private sector, but also that the state should intervene less through the imposition of planning regulations and controls. ... While no-one who has studied state intervention in the housing market in Latin America will regret a certain rolling back of its role, the current statements from Washington sound all too much like 'trickle-down' economics.

Will the benefits really reach the majority of the poor?

It is possible that this approach will be effective in the expanding economies of the region. If poor people find work and their incomes start to rise, then they will be able to improve the quality of their homes. If more and cheaper credit is made available, the operation of land and housing markets may well improve to everyone's benefit. If government, or increasingly private enterprise, invests in sensible projects, the quality and availability of infrastructure and services may improve for increasing numbers of low-income settlers. But so much depends on continued economic growth and on its more equitable distribution. In the region's declining economies, or those where the distribution of income continues to deteriorate, market forces will not help poor families to improve their shelter. Not only does economic decline cut family budgets, but it also undermines the ability of governments to supply services. Self-help settlement with water, electricity and sewage is one thing; its development without such basic amenities is hardly to be commended. It is an unfortunate fact that during the economic recession of the 1980s many governments cut back investment in just this area of activity. It remains to be seen whether the experience of the 1990s will be significantly better. (Gilbert, 1994, pp. 100–1)

(See also Drakakis-Smith, 1986; Edel and Hellman, 1989; Gilbert, 1986; Harriss and Moore, 1984; Portes, 1989; PREALC, 1990c; Priestley, 1989; Pryor and Crook, 1988; Safa, 1987 and Schaefer, 1976.)

3.7 Conclusions

In this chapter, we have examined a number of problems affecting those who work in the UIS.

First, *poverty* was considered and the evidence suggested that there was no simple, causal link between poverty and working in the UIS, though proportionately more UIS than UFS workers were found among the poor. It appeared that *vulnerability* was an important factor and that this related to age, lack of education (or skills) and the number of dependents within a household. Since the vulnerable are found in both sectors, it is clear that formalising the UIS will not in itself reduce the problem of poverty.

Secondly, gender differences were highlighted by disaggregating earnings data by sex, which showed that generally women earn less than men within the same occupational group. Further analysis suggested that *segmentation* of the labour market, through cultural and familial views of appropriate 'female' and 'male' jobs, was more important than simple sexual *discrimination* in explaining the differentials. One link back to the discussion of poverty was the high proportion of female-headed multiperson households among the very poor. Chilean data revealed that such households had more dependents than corresponding male-headed households, a factor that correlates positively with extreme poverty.

Thirdly, the role of *children* in the UIS was highlighted. Despite the fact that most countries have signed international conventions banning child labour in many activities, poverty forces many children to work from a young age. Many combine part-time work with obtaining an education, but there is some bias here against girls, who are often required to spend time at home looking after younger siblings in order to allow adult females to go out to work. A particularly vulnerable group are those children who both work and live in the streets, since in some countries they have been subject to torture and murder by extreme right-wing groups, although governments are being put under pressure from international and national human-rights groups to protect them.

Fourthly, the possibility of extending *social protection* to the UIS was considered and it was shown that, despite the fact that existing social insurance schemes in many Latin American countries were narrow in coverage they worked very badly and inefficiently. As a result, it was generally not feasible to extend them to include the UIS. At best the poor within the UIS might be reached through appropriate general subsidies or specific targeting and the trade-off between these two approaches was discussed.

Finally, since migration played a key role in the rapid urbanisation following World War II, the way in which the migrants 'solved' the housing shortage through *squatting and self-help housing* was explored. It was shown that under the influence of international organisations (especially the World Bank) governments have moved from their early attitudes that squatter settlements were 'blots on the landscape' to the more positive role of taking part in upgrading existing settlements and site-and-services programmes. These programmes have been targeted to specific needs and have improved the housing standards of squatters, though whether they reach the poorest of the poor is open to question as is how they will fare in the current neo-liberal free-market climate in Latin America.

Although they are not identical groups, it is clear that many UIS workers are poor, are not protected by social insurance, live in bad housing and, in the case of women, may be particularly

103

vulnerable. In the past, these disadvantages were ignored or treated with indifference by the rest of society – the rich person getting into an expensive car and giving a few small coins to the child that has cleaned and guarded it is a common sight in many Latin American cities. Many of those working in the informal sector (such as street vendors and others operating in public view) were visible to those who chose to see. However, in terms of their needs and potential contributions to the economy, they have tended to be invisible to the authorities and existed only as statistics on birth or death certificates, if even that.

Recently, some things have changed and the UIS has attracted positive attention both from those who see its importance in soaking up surplus labour which cannot be absorbed by the UFS, and from those who see in the bureaucracy-free UIS the potential to act as the engine of economic growth. Regardless of which (if either) of these views one takes, a number of questions arise concerning the future of the UIS. First, what predictions may be made concerning its development in coming years; will it increase or decrease as a percentage of the urban EAP? Secondly, if one takes a positive view of helping those in the UIS, what policies and programmes are likely to be useful? We shall turn to these questions in the next chapter.

4 The Future of the Urban Informal Sector

4.1 *The Future of the UIS: Growth or Decline?*

Given the current world recession and the effects of the debt crisis, the 1980s in Latin America has been called 'the lost decade'. The data presented in Chapter 2 show that the UIS increased in size in most Latin American countries during that period, absorbing many of the new entrants into the labour force as well as those driven out of the UFS by the recession and structural adjustment programmes. In the last few years there have been signs in at least some countries that the debt crisis has eased and that real growth has begun. If this process continues and spreads to most countries in the region, what is likely to happen to the UIS first in the short run and secondly in the long run?

Short-run prospects
One exploration of the short-run prospects for the UIS was made by PREALC (1990e), which presents the results of simulation experiments exploring the likely effects of alternative scenarios on ten countries that together represented more than 95 per cent of the urban EAP and employment in Latin America. These were classified into four groups on the basis of (a) whether the rate of growth of the urban EAP was below or above the average for the ten countries and (b) on whether the country had undertaken a low or high degree of structural adjustment (see Table 4.1 below).

Two economic variables played an important role in the simulations: (i) the percentage of GDP that had to be transferred abroad to service the debt and (ii) the rate of growth of exports, which in structural adjustment programmes played a crucial role in the move towards export orientated growth. In Scenario I, the Basic simulation, it was assumed that the share of GDP being transferred abroad would fall from 3.8 per cent in the late 1980s to 2.8 per cent in the year 2000. The second assumption was that the rate of increase in exports would be 5.1 per cent per annum over the same period. Scenario II, the Rapid Growth simulation,

Table 4.1 *Classification of Latin American Countries by Growth of Urban EAP and Degree of Structural Adjustment*

Growth of Urban EAP	Degree of structural adjustment	
	Low	High
	Group A:	Group B:
Below average	Argentina	Chile
	Uruguay	Colombia
		Costa Rica
	Group C:	Group D:
Above average	Peru	Brazil
	Guatemala	Mexico
		Venezuela

Source: Based on PREALC (1990e), p. 62.

assumed that the fall in the transfer of GDP abroad would be from 3.8 per cent to 1.4 per cent and that the rate of increase in exports would be 6.4 per cent per annum.

These values were introduced into an economic model in order to examine their effects on employment and the relative growth in the UIS and the UFS. Being a short-run simulation, only a limited amount of technological change and increased capital intensity can be expected in the period considered. One would expect that under Scenario II, with less GDP being needed to service the debt, more would be available to stimulate growth. Similarly, imposing the higher export rate on an 'export-led growth' model would lead to higher growth than under Scenario I. This is indeed the case for the ten countries taken together; under Scenario I, the percentage of the urban EAP in the UIS grows from 31.4 per cent in 1991 to 34.0 per cent in 1995 and to 35.6 per cent in 2000; for Scenario II the corresponding percentages are 31.4 per cent in 1991, 33.2 per cent in 1995 and 32.9 per cent in 2000. Thus, even the highly optimistic scenario predicts that the UIS would have increased its share in the urban EAP by the year 2000.

Examining the four groups of countries in Table 4.1 separately under the two scenarios, the important factor in the simulations is the rate of growth of the urban EAP. Groups A and B, whose growth was below the ten-country average, both showed decreases in the share of the UIS in the urban EAP, these being larger under Scenario II than Scenario I. Group B, the group farther along with structural adjustment, showed bigger falls than Group A under both scenarios. Conversely, both Groups C and D showed increases in the share of the UIS in the urban EAP under both scenarios, but these were larger under Scenario I than Scenario II for both groups and the effect was smaller for Group D than for Group C under both scenarios.

Alternative economic models would have given different numerical results, but the finding that the rate of increase of the urban EAP is more important than the stage of structural adjustment in determining the growth of the UIS is robust and has important policy implications. In general, rates of migration to the cities of Latin America have decreased in recent years. However, urban population continues to grow (even if at a lower rate) as a result of high birthrates among poor families, where a *machismo* culture and the Catholic Church obstruct women's access to family planning (see Harper, 1992).

Long-run prospects
These are more difficult to predict, but must be affected by the worldwide development of increasingly capital-intensive technology, which has implications for developed as well as for developing countries. The UNDP chose as the symbol for the cover of the *Human Development Report 1993* a graph of two indices to illustrate the disturbing phenomenon of jobless growth during the latter part of the twentieth century. One index showed regional GDP for the world growing from 100 in 1975 and 156 in 1990 to a projected value of 205 in 2000. The other index showed world employment growing from 100 in 1975 and 128 in 1990 to a projected 147 in 2000. The disturbing feature of the graph was that the gap between the two indices widened after 1990; in other words, the projected level of GDP would be produced with proportionately less labour.

These indices are regionally weighted, so the dominant effect being caught is the growth performances in the OECD countries, which include the EU. Many EU countries have had high levels of unemployment that have fallen only very slowly. Some workers, especially unskilled men in their fifties, have been unemployed for years and are unlikely to get jobs again even when growth in aggregate output returns. Many school leavers have been unable to find work and, but for government training schemes, would have been unemployed. The effect of neo-liberal economic policies in many countries has been a process of deregulation and privatisation, with an increasing 'informalisation' leading to the employment of more part-time workers (especially women) and sub-contracting (see Portes, Castells and Benton, 1989).

The possible long-term effects of neo-liberal policies in Latin America have to be seen against a very different demographic background to that existing in the OECD countries. Table 4.2 contains a summary of demographic trends in Latin America from 1970 to 1992. The data reveal some marked differences between countries, with some countries showing very high Total Fertility Rates (TFR), high Infant Mortality Rates (IMR) and low Life Expectancies at Birth (LEB), but the dominant picture is that there are clear and similar trends for all the countries.

1. The TFR declined in all countries over the period, though the rate of decline varies across countries and has been very small in some. Decreasing fertility rates would, *ceteris paribus*,[1] tend to reduce pressure on the labour market through a reduction in the number of job seekers.

2. All countries have experienced falls in the IMR, which have been much more dramatic than the declines in TFR. This operates in the opposite direction to the effect of decreases in TFR, as declining IMRs mean that, *ceteris paribus*, more children survive to join the labour force and put a downward pressure on earnings.

3. The LEB has increased in all countries, so that, *ceteris paribus*, there will be more old people in all Latin American countries in the future. Given the poor provision of social benefits and pensions in most Latin American countries, old people who are poor will have to support themselves and will need to work in their old age, since they are unlikely to be able to afford to buy the benefits provided by private pension schemes.

On balance, the trends show that fewer children are being born on average to each mother, but an increasing proportion of those are surviving beyond their first year. If we treat these as independent factors, they have opposite effects on future increases in the labour force. However, it is possible that parents may eventually react to

---

1. Economists use the Latin term *ceteris paribus*, which means "all things being equal" to analyse situations in which one variable is changed while the others are held constant. This is a convenient way of isolating and then combining the effects of a number of changes which may work in different directions.

Table 4.2 *Demographic Trends in Latin America, 1970–92*

Country	Year				
	1970	1975	1980	1985	1992
Argentina					
TFR	3.1	3.3	3.4	3.2	2.8
IMR	51.8	44.2	38.0	30.1	29.0
LEB	66.8	68.1	69.3	70.3	71.4
Bolivia					
TFR	6.5	6.4	6.3	6.1	4.7
IMR	153.4	143.2	129.6	119.6	82.0
LEB	46.1	47.9	49.9	52.7	59.6
Brazil					
TFR	4.9	4.4	4.0	3.6	2.8
IMR	94.6	83.8	74.2	57.2	57.0
LEB	59.0	61.0	62.8	62.5	66.2
Chile					
TFR	4.0	3.2	2.8	2.6	2.7
IMR	82.2	57.5	33.0	24.9	17.0
LEB	62.4	65.7	69.5	71.3	72.0
Colombia					
TFR	5.3	4.0	3.5	3.3	2.7
IMR	79.0	66.0	58.0	48.8	21.0
LEB	59.1	61.0	63.1	65.0	69.3
Ecuador					
TFR	6.3	5.7	5.2	4.6	3.5
IMR	99.8	87.2	74.8	54.8	45.0
LEB	58.1	60.4	63.1	65.3	66.6
Paraguay					
TFR	6.0	5.3	4.9	4.7	4.6
IMR	58.6	50.6	46.6	43.4	35.5
LEB	65.3	65.8	66.3	66.6	67.2
Peru					
TFR	6.0	5.3	4.7	4.2	3.3
IMR	116.4	107.0	101.4	79.6	52.0
LEB	53.9	56.4	57.9	60.0	64.6
Uruguay					
TFR	2.9	3.0	2.8	2.7	2.3
IMR	47.4	45.2	35.6	27.5	20.0
LEB	68.8	69.3	70.1	70.8	72.4

continued

Table 4.2 *continued*

Country	Year				
	1970	*1975*	*1980*	*1985*	*1992*
Venezuela					
TFR	5.3	4.7	4.2	3.9	3.6
IMR	53.4	45.4	40.6	33.1	33.0
LEB	65.2	67.1	68.5	69.6	70.3
Costa Rica					
TFR	4.9	3.9	3.6	3.4	3.1
IMR	61.5	37.8	20.1	17.4	14.0
LEB	67.1	69.0	71.7	73.4	76.3
El Salvador					
TFR	6.3	5.9	5.4	5.0	3.8
IMR	103.0	88.0	74.8	65.3	40.0
LEB	57.6	57.9	57.3	60.2	66.3
Guatemala					
TFR	6.5	6.4	6.2	5.9	5.1
IMR	100.2	87.2	74.8	67.3	62.0
LEB	52.5	55.4	58.0	60.3	64.8
Honduras					
TFR	7.4	6.9	6.3	5.8	4.9
IMR	115.2	101.0	87.2	64.8	49.0
LEB	52.7	56.2	60.2	63.2	65.8
Nicaragua					
TFR	6.9	6.5	6.1	5.7	4.4
IMR	106.0	95.8	82.8	68.9	56.0
LEB	53.5	55.7	58.4	60.8	66.6
Panama					
TFR	5.2	4.4	3.7	3.3	2.9
IMR	46.6	36.4	28.4	23.9	21.0
LEB	65.5	68.1	70.3	71.5	72.8
Dominican Republic					
TFR	6.0	5.1	4.4	3.9	3.0
IMR	98.4	88.0	78.6	56.8	41.0
LEB	58.7	61.2	63.3	65.3	67.5
Mexico					
TFR	6.5	5.5	4.5	3.8	3.2
IMR	73.0	63.6	55.8	42.0	35.0
LEB	61.7	64.3	66.6	68.1	70.3

continued

Table 4.2 *continued*

Country	Year				
	1970	1975	1980	1985	1992
UK					
TFR	2.4	1.8	1.9	1.8	1.8
IMR	18.5	16.0	12.1	12.9	7.0
LEB	71.7	72.4	73.8	74.5	76.2
USA					
TFR	2.5	1.8	1.8	1.3	2.1
IMR	20.0	16.1	12.6	9.4	8.6
LEB	70.8	72.6	73.7	74.8	76.6

Source: *World Tables*, 1988–89 Edition and 1994 Edition. (NB figures for 1992 are estimates.)

Key:
TFR: Total Fertility Rate = average number of children that would be born to a woman during her lifetime if she were to bear children at each age in accordance with prevailing age-specific fertility rates.
IMR: Infant Mortality Rate = number of infants per thousand live births, in a given year, who die before reaching one year of age.
LEB: Life Expectancy at Birth = number of years a newborn infant would live if prevailing patterns of mortality for all people at the time of birth were to stay the same throughout his or her life.

the increased probability of a child surviving by having fewer children and this could increase the rate of decline in the TFR.

The neo-liberal path has been urged upon the countries of Latin America and is already being followed by some. The result may well be similar to that observed in the developed countries, with a weakening of trade unions and changes in the structure of jobs in the UFS towards more 'flexible' labour contracts, as well as decreases in the size of the public sector as the state withdraws from economic activity and civil servants are 'retrenched'.

To the extent that the countries in Latin America follow similar economic trends to those captured in the UNDP indices, one would predict increasing capital intensity in UFS production and proportionately fewer UFS jobs. Unless the urban EAP grows more slowly in the future, or there is an offsetting increase in rural employment opportunities to draw urban population to the countryside, there will be increasing pressure on the UIS to absorb the 'surplus' urban labour force.

If the predictions are correct and the UIS continues to expand, can anything be done to improve the position of those in the sector during this process? Since there are two sides to every transaction, one may divide policies relating to the UIS into those relating to the supply-side, and those that are concerned with the demand for the output from the UIS.

Two factors that have been seen as important supply-side constraints on the operation of the UIS are lack of education and training, and lack of access to credit and opportunities to save (see Bowles, 1988). These will be discussed in Sections 4.2 and 4.3 below.

If the output of the UIS expands, then there must be a corresponding expansion in demand if the prices of the goods and services produced in the UIS are not to fall because of excess supply. A number of proposals for expanding demand for UIS output are considered in Section 4.4.

4.2 *Supply-side Measures: Education and Training*

As Tables 2.4 and 2.5 above show, workers in the UIS have less education than those in the UFS. In addition, generally in Latin America, women have lower literacy rates and fewer years of education than men (see UNDP, 1993, pp. 144–5, Table 5). While all children are formally required to attend at least primary school, it is clear that many poor children are only able to study part-time, if at all. Educationally, many in the UIS are disadvantaged as compared with those in the UFS.

There has long been recognition, at least on the part of international organisations, of the need for education or training appropriate for those working in the UIS. Indeed the ILO's mission to Kenya (ILO, 1972) criticised the quality of primary education at the time on the grounds that it ignored the needs of the majority of pupils by preparing them for secondary schools instead of for work in rural areas and in the informal sector. However, this awareness was not immediately translated into action by governments.

One problem is that many of those in the UIS who have little formal education are not aware of the benefits they might obtain from further education or training and hence do not demand it. Ministries of Education are under pressure from those in the UFS for other kinds of education and the resources tend to go there. As King (1989) points out:

By contrast, workers in the informal sector do not appear to be putting any pressure on the education and training systems for more provision. In one way, they share a characteristic that is common to much adult education – they need to be *persuaded* to become clients of education or further training. In a situation where ministries and their political masters are faced by one set of clients demanding more high schools, colleges and universities, and another set who are apparently somewhat resistant to further training, it is not difficult to understand the budgetary outcome. In some countries, less than 1 per cent of the recurrent budget of the Ministry of Education goes to the area of adult, nonformal education and training, which gives some indication of the balance between provision for adults as compared with school and college students. (p. 18)

There have been some notable exceptions, such as Colombia's National Apprenticeship Service (SENA), which was set up to provide training for the UFS, 'but "discovered" the informal sector as early as the 1960s' (Ramírez, 1989, p. 161). However, many of the early programmes were developed by NGOs, such as the Carvajal Foundation, a Colombian NGO based in the city of Cali (see Carvajal, 1989 and Harper, 1989; see also Haan, 1989b and Ramírez, 1989 for a survey of other Latin American programmes). Now one finds both governments and NGOs involved, often working in close cooperation (see Stearns and Otero, 1990 and Otero, 1994).

The range of training courses is wide. This reflects in part the different approaches that have been taken on questions such as day release to attend courses versus on-the-job training. It also reflects the heterogeneity of the UIS (see Fluitman, 1989). The poor literacy rates and low educational levels of many of those in the UIS present difficulties to the trainers and those to be trained. Solutions range from giving potential students a preliminary course in basic literacy and numeracy before the training programme to providing training material that is designed for people with low levels of literacy, for example by making use of illustrations and cartoon strip presentations of material.

As was shown in Chapter 3, there is considerable segmentation within the UIS, with women tending to be self-employed and occupied in commerce and services or working as unpaid family workers.[2] Men are more heavily represented in manufacturing,

---

2. There are a number of problems with training programmes concerning time and location that particularly affect women's participation. These will be discussed in the next section.

especially among entrepreneurs. The result has been that training programmes aiming to help microenterprises improve their efficiency in order to give them the opportunity of moving into the UFS have tended to concentrated on these enterprises. There is little evidence of much success in this process; studies of training programmes suggest that after training microenterprises may operate more efficiently, but they are still close to their original size, with little growth having occurred (see McKee, 1988).

4.3 *Supply-side Measures: Savings and Credit*

To many observers, a major constraint on the UIS is the lack of access people in the sector have to credit. For example, the working capital of self-employed workers in commerce or services is often very limited, with the result that they have to purchase their basic materials frequently and in small quantities from retailers, rather than in larger quantities from wholesalers at lower prices. Similarly, microenterprises may be constrained to work with primitive technology as they do not have access to the funds required to buy better tools or machinery.

What causes this lack of access to credit? The major cause is the lack of contact, both physical and social, between those working in the UIS and the commercial banking system. First, because of the small scale of business in the UIS, most transactions are carried out in cash and few of those in the sector have need to use cheques or bank accounts. Secondly, given the suspicions of the middle classes that many of those operating in the UIS are involved in various criminal activities, commercial banks do not seek out business with the sector; the banks do not have branch offices in the poor areas where those in the UIS tend to live and workers in the UIS are not welcome in the banks' downtown branches.

To obtain credit a borrower must (a) convince the bank of the economic soundness of the investment and (b) provide assurances as to his or her financial probity. The first requirement may involve the bank in an evaluation of the economic risk involved in carrying out the proposal. The second requirement, involving an evaluation of the customer's ability to repay the loan, may be satisfied either through credit worthiness or collateral (or both).

Credit worthiness and transaction costs
A long-term customer has had an opportunity to build up a relationship of trust with the bank over time. However, in the absence of such contact, the bank may have to carry out a special investigation

of the customer's financial affairs as well as evaluate the merits of the investment. As the size of loans required by those in the UIS is small, the fixed costs of the evaluations are large in relation to the loan, with the result that bank charges would have to be high in order to cover costs.

The problem of collateral

Absence of credit worthiness can be compensated for if the potential borrower has marketable assets that can be offered as collateral for the loan, in which case the bank will not lose financially if the borrower is unable or unwilling to repay the loan. In this respect, those working in the UIS are at a disadvantage as they own little of commercial value to the banks. For example, while some of the more successful microenterprises may own plant or equipment that has sufficient value to be used as collateral, for many it is likely to be obsolete and of little market value. The possibility of using one's home as collateral is ruled out, as the market value of a shanty dwelling constructed out of cardboard and other industrial waste in a marginal squatter settlement is hardly likely to provide desirable collateral to a commercial bank.

Social collateral and group-solidarity credit programmes

One solution to the problem that the poor do not own marketable collateral is to substitute something else in its place. Muhammad Yunus proposed and implemented a credit programme to help poor women in rural Bangladesh by founding the Grameen Bank in 1973 (see Yunus, 1989). In place of the physical collateral, which the women did not possess, Yunus substituted *social collateral*, that is a system under which loans were made to members of small groups who took responsibility for each other's loans.

The first step in obtaining a loan is for the women to negotiate amongst themselves to form groups of five persons to whom the loan would be made. Since the women know each other and who would or would not be willing and able to repay the loan, making the women form the groups taps into local knowledge and reduces the risk of default to the bank.

The second step is that the five loans are made as a group loan; if any one member of the group defaults all members of the group are penalised. This activates the *group-solidarity* in the programme, as the women have a strong incentive to ensure that all members of the group repay on time. This may involve the women applying sanctions or support to the potential non-repayee, depending on the reason for the potential default.

The Grameen Bank is widely regarded as being successful, as it

115

obtains repayment rates of over 95 per cent and charges a rate of interest that is high enough to cover the costs of the programme, but is lower than that charged by local money lenders. Given its success, it has been used as the model for credit programmes in other areas, including the UIS in Latin America (see USAID, 1985a,b; Ashe, 1986; Beltrán, 1988; Lycette and White, 1989 and Thomas, 1993b).

Combining training and credit
While some programmes only provide credit, others provide business training as well as lending. For some, such as IDESI, the Peruvian institution that provides credit to workers in the UIS, taking and passing the training courses is a prerequisite for those wishing to obtain credit in the programme (see Pinilla, 1986).

The main reason for combining these two activities is the view that those who wish to borrow may not have sufficient business skills to be able to manage a loan, whereas after learning the rudiments of stock control and book keeping they are in a better position to cope with increased financial commitments and handling larger quantities. An account of the experience of a Colombian shoe-maker involved in the combined training and credit programme run by the Carvajal Foundation in Cali is given in Box 4.1.

While there are arguments in favour of providing training along with credit, there is no clear agreement on the best way to combine them. For example, should both be provided by the same organisation, or should the providers of credit sub-contract the training to experts in that area? While in practice many credit programmes have provided their own training components, there are some advantages to sub-contracting.

First, those involved in running a credit programme (particularly when it is being set up) may not have the expertise to provide a good training component in the programme. It may be more efficient for them to make use of existing training organisations that have been tried and tested and have the experience to tailor courses to suit borrowers in credit programmes.

Secondly, given the heterogeneity of the UIS, they may not be able to offer a wide enough range of training courses in-house to suit all borrowers. For example, self-employed women who are involved in commerce or services may not need the same kind of training that would be appropriate for an entrepreneur running a microenterprise (see Goodale, 1989a,b; Placencia, 1989 and Bourque and Warren, 1990). If the costs of training are recovered in the interest charged on the loan, such women would be penalised financially if required to undertake and pay for unsuitable training.

Box 4.1 Training and Credit for a Colombian Shoe-maker

Don Fernando makes women's shoes and sandals in a workshop behind his home. He employs two helpers and has a stitching machine and some simple hand tools. He makes fashionable shoes of modern design which he sells mainly to large shopkeepers in the centre of Cali. He achieves a turnover of around US$500 a month and he believes he could sell perhaps twice this amount if he had more working capital.

Fernando's current working capital amounts to some US$180, which is all invested in raw materials and semi-finished goods. As soon as he has finished a batch of shoes, he takes them to the customers; they pay with cheques which are post-dated by two or three months and Fernando has to discount these at around 8 per cent per month in order to obtain cash. Although he could borrow more money at this rate of interest, he does not feel he can afford the cost.

Fernando has taken the record-keeping and costing courses from DESAP and is currently working with his advisor to find ways of reducing his costs and getting better results from his working capital. He hopes to proceed to the investment planning course and then apply for a US$1,000 loan. He knows he will have to pay 24 per cent interest per year, but this is far cheaper than 8 per cent per month and he is confident that he will be able to hire two more helpers and significantly increase his own earnings.

Fernando admits that his main motive for entering the DESAP Programme was to obtain a loan, since other sources of credit are quite inaccessible to him. He recognises however, that he has learned a great deal from the two courses he has attended and from the individual counselling, and is looking forward to the third course. He agrees that if he had been able to borrow US$1,000 without first taking the course, he might easily have failed to make effective use of the additional capital and thus have put himself in an even worse position than before.

Source: Direct quotation from Harper (1989), p. 178.

Thirdly, making training compulsory may cause problems for potential women borrowers whose time is scarce. As McKean (1994) notes:

Time is a constraint to the firm owner's ability to benefit from training and technical assistance services. ... In particular, it would be difficult for women who manage both a business and a household to find the time to attend three weeks of required

117

coursework, a fact verified by an evaluation of the small business credit program of the Industrial Bank of Peru. (p. 211)

There is clearly a need for flexibility here, particularly in programmes that aim to help women working in the UIS. It is not obvious that a great deal of training is needed for some of the activities performed by women in commerce and services at the beginning of the programme, but if the credit increases their motivation to expand business or change their activities, further training may be appropriate to facilitate their new plans. It is particularly important to involve members of credit programmes in structuring the package of training and credit, rather than imposing a narrow programme upon them.

A number of studies to evaluate the success of various credit programmes agree that many of them attain high repayment rates, cover their costs and are self-sustaining. However, it is more difficult to evaluate how much good they have done to the recipients (see Buvinic, Berger and Jaramillo, 1989; Christen, 1989; Mezzera, 1987, 1993; Otero, 1989a,b; PREALC, 1990a; Reichmann, 1989; Stearns, 1991 and Thomas, 1993b,c).

First, the Grameen Bank model is geared to giving small loans for short periods. This works better with working capital than with capital investments, which usually require larger amounts over longer periods of time. Thus Grameen Bank style programmes aimed at helping those (mainly women) working in commerce have been more successful than those geared to helping entrepreneurs (mainly men) in manufacturing.

Secondly, criteria for evaluating programmes may not be consistent with the objects of the programme. For example, many programmes have specifically targeted women, but have taken increases in the number of paid employees as one criterion for judging the success of the programme. However, this ignores the evidence that a high proportion of women in credit programmes are currently self-employed or work with unpaid family help, whereas men form a higher proportion of entrepreneurs who hire paid employees. The moral is that if the programme is to help women, it is not very useful to look for increases in paid employment in the early phases of the programme; it would be more relevant to look for increases in the woman's income and perhaps the living standard of her family.[3]

---

3. There are many technical problems regarding the need for control groups when evaluating the effects of credit programmes that are being ignored here (see Thomas, 1993c).

To summarise, credit programmes that have offered small loans are seen as having been successful, particularly in providing credit to poor women. Providing credit to microenterprises has tended to be more difficult and has faced more risk, with higher default rates. While such loans have encouraged some increases in paid employment, there is little evidence that there has been significant growth in the size of microenterprises as a result of the programmes.

While credit programmes are generally regarded positively as 'doing good for the poor', they are mostly unable to reach the poorest of the poor because of the need for financial viability. As Márquez (1994) notes:

> most informal sector programs in Latin America deliver credit and support to the less poor among the informal sector workers. This is not the result of social callousness among these organizations, but the implicit outcome of pressures for sustainability. Credit must be repaid. By focusing assistance on more viable activities, lenders increase their chances of becoming financially self-sustaining (and miss targeting the poorest informals). (p. 167)

Most of the credit programmes in Latin America have been run by NGOs rather than by government agencies. Although there is a case for governments to become more involved in funding and running such programmes, a more important role is to exercise monetary control so that inflation is kept under control. For example, most of the NGOs operating credit programmes in Peru had to cut back their activities sharply during 1988–90 as it was extremely difficult to obtain adequate repayments in real terms from borrowers during the hyperinflation of 1989–90.

Savings
Contrary to popular belief, the poor can save and try to do so (see Remenyi, 1991), even though the amounts are often tiny and the turnover is very rapid. Those higher up the income scale within the UIS sometimes have resources in excess of immediate needs and wish to save. One of the features of the original Grameen Bank was that borrowers were required to save with the Bank. This had the effect of giving the borrower a stake in the Bank and reducing the risk of default, but also provided a channel for saving that was secure. The banking laws in most Latin American countries that cover borrowing from the public do not include credit programmes. As a result, they are not allowed to take deposits from their mem-

119

bers and so the savings component is missing from such programmes. This leaves many in the UIS without a means of saving that could provide flexibility in handling small amounts of money for very short periods.

4.4 *Increasing the Demand for the Output of the UIS*

What determines the demand for the output from the UIS? A simple question, but one to which we do not have an answer, as research on the UIS has not explored this question in a systematic way. We know that part of the output of the UIS is an input into the UFS through sub-contracting, but data on the proportion of UIS output involved is sketchy. The rest of the output of the UIS goes to the final consumer, but there is very little information on the distribution of consumers between the UIS and the UFS.

One study that provides information on the demand for the output from the UIS is Grosskoff and Melgar (1990). This study is based on a survey of 1,290 households carried out in Montevideo in 1982–83. The survey not only collected data on household expenditure, but also obtained sufficient additional data to identify whether the goods and services were purchased from the UFS or from the UIS. The authors defined four categories of output.

Category 1 Goods and services produced in the UFS and sold predominantly by that sector (e.g. some foodstuffs, clothing, consumer durables, expenditure on housing and health, etc.).

Category 2 Goods and services produced in the UFS and sold by both the UFS and the UIS (e.g. foodstuffs bought from street-sellers, clothing, furniture, etc.).

Category 3 Goods and services produced and sold with an important participation by the UIS (e.g. services, such as dyeing and laundering clothing, such as hats, scarves and belts, etc.).

Category 4 Goods and services both produced and sold by the UIS (e.g. personal services, such as hairdressing, dressmaking and tailoring, repairing domestic objects, artisan products, etc.).

Table 4.3 presents the percentages of the four categories purchased by households, classified into deciles by consumpion expenditure, and illustrates the importance of the UIS as a distributor of the output of the UFS (Category 2), particularly in the lower deciles.

At first sight the increasing percentage of expenditure on Category 4 items by decile may be surprising, but a closer examination reveals that the major item here is furniture – artisan furniture can be very trendy.

In addition to having little information on the structure of demand for the output of the UIS, there is also little information on what has been happening to this demand over time, particularly during the difficult period of the 1980s.

Some researchers have estimated what has happened to the demand for the output of the UIS. For example, PREALC (1991a) present data to show that an index of real wages for medium and large sized enterprises based on seven Latin American (Argentina, Brazil, Chile, Colombia, Costa Rica, Mexico and Venezuela) fell by 0.8 per cent between 1980 and 1989. During that period, the numbers working in the UIS rose by 72 per cent. On the assumption that the total demand for the output of the UIS came from the UFS and was at best constant, it was assumed that since demand was fixed, the average income in the UIS fell in proportion to the numbers of workers in the UIS, i.e. by 42 per cent. This is based on an extreme assumption that there is no substitution between goods and services produced in the UIS and the UFS.

Table 4.3 *The Demand for Output from the UFS and UIS in Montevideo, 1982–83*

Decile	Category				Total
	1	2	3	4	
1	55.3	43.6	0.8	0.3	100.0
2	56.5	41.7	0.9	0.9	100.0
3	58.0	39.3	1.2	1.5	100.0
4	60.0	37.0	1.0	2.0	100.0
5	59.0	38.0	1.4	1.6	100.0
6	57.1	38.9	1.3	2.7	100.0
7	60.1	34.8	2.1	3.0	100.0
8	58.9	35.2	2.3	3.6	100.0
9	60.4	29.8	4.1	5.7	100.0
10	65.3	25.9	2.1	6.7	100.0
Average	60.3	33.8	2.0	3.9	100.0

Source: Based on Grosskoff and Melgar (1990), p. 191, Table 7.
Key: For Deciles 1 = poorest and 10 = richest. For Categories, see text for definition.

It seems more likely that there will be some substitution of the cheaper goods produced in the UIS for those produced in the UFS and if this is so, then the PREALC calculation may be an overestimate of the effect of cuts in UFS employment on UIS income. As there is little empirical evidence on the structure of demand for the UIS, it is difficult to resolve this issue. The lack of information regarding the distribution of the output of the UIS also makes it difficult to evaluate proposals to increase sectoral demand.

At the macroeconomic level, two policies have been proposed to increase the demand for UIS output: positive discrimination by the state towards the UIS, and increased sub-contracting from the UFS to the UIS.

Positive discrimination towards the UIS
Government attitudes towards intervening in favour of the UIS in Latin America have changed, becoming more positive over time (see Otero, 1994). While some countries have become actively involved in playing a direct role (Colombia for example), most have encouraged other agencies, such as NGOs, to intervene through training and credit programmes of the kind discussed in the previous sections, i.e. supply-side intervention.

However, some NGOs are aware of the need to expand markets if supply-side measures are to work and they conduct market analyses as part of the programmes. For example, de Wilde, Schreurs and Richman (1991) present a detailed case study of a programme to encourage the production of wheelchairs by microenterprises in Colombia. Here it was found that a credit scheme was necessary to enable potential disabled customers to purchase the chairs. Having bought them, they were able to work and generate the income to pay off the loans. This credit element in the programme generated the demand necessary for the output of wheelchairs to expand. The authors report (p. 11) that during the period 1984–87 the NGO Appropriate Technology International used some type of consumer financing for the products of more than 1,200 microenterprises in order to create or expand demand (see also Harper and Ramachandran, 1984).

In many Latin American countries, microenterprises have been encouraged to join existing trade associations or create their own. The objective is to co-operate in publicising the goods being produced (for example, through trade fairs and displays) and extend the size of the market (see Villarán, 1993, on Peru).

Another form of positive discrimination that has been discussed is for the state to restructure public sector purchasing towards the UIS. There are problems here, since producers in the UIS cannot supply the large quantities of standardised goods that are required if public expenditure is highly centralised. However, a policy of decentralisation of public expenditure to the municipal level may make it easier to direct demand towards the UIS. PRE-ALC (1990d) reports a case study of the deregulation of educational expenditure in São Paulo that suggested that about 20 per cent of the employment created in educational construction and maintenance through decentralisation took place in the UIS.

However, such examples are still uncommon and the main avenue that has been suggested for expanding UIS demand is through sub-contracting.

Sub-contracting and the UIS

As we saw in Chapter 2, sub-contracting already exists as an important link between the UIS and the UFS and there are different views on whether or not it constitutes a form of exploitation. For those who take a positive view of this economic link, the state could encourage the activity through public purchasing by favouring those UFS firms that sub-contracted work to the UIS. Alternatively, sub-contracting may well increase anyway, as governments adopt neo-liberal free-market policies and explicity or implicity encourage UFS firms to avoid 'market distortions', such as minimum wage legislation, trade union negotiations, rigid labour contracts, health and safety regulations and other costs by 'informalising' their business operations. This may involve making more use of part-time or short contract workers and sub-contracting to the UIS.

This process may be described as *top-down* informality, where the initiative may come from UFS firms:

> with a neo-liberal perception of 'flexibility', i.e. the need to maintain their competitive edge in times of crisis, cutting labour and jettisoning social costs, among others, by sub-contracting part of the goods and services they themselves previously produced. (CEDEFOP, 1993, p. 31.)

This may be contrasted with *bottom-up* informality, which has to do with survival and creating work in the absence of UFS alternatives.

Even viewing the benefits to the UIS of subcontracting positively, it is important to consider whether an increase in such sub-contracting takes place in a situation of growing demand or static demand for UFS output. If the former, it may be profitable for the firms to expand output through a combination of sub-contracting and increased UFS production, which would tend to maintain employment in the UFS. If demand is static, then the 'flexibility' argument may lead to a substitution of sub-contracting for direct production in the UFS and the shedding of UFS jobs. These workers may well be forced into the UIS, possibly as part of the 'bottom-up' process of survival.

In ILO (1991a), the Director-General of the ILO, Michel Hansenne, voiced the concern experienced by those working to improve the contractual and physical conditions of workers during a period in which the previous gains, in terms of minimum wage legislation and social insurance, were now being lost through de-regulation and the weakened position of trade unions. Far from welcoming the removal of all regulations, as advocated by de Soto, Hansenne expressed concern over the future expansion of the UIS under neo-liberal conditions:

> For the ILO, the existence of a large and growing informal sector presents as much of a dilemma as it does for its member States. We need to look to the informal sector as the only possible source of employment for increasing numbers of the developing world's rapidly growing labour force, and to help our member States to increase its dynamism and its capacity to absorb more and more labour. At the same time, we cannot turn a blind eye to the fact that the standards and principles which constitute the very reason for the ILO's existence are not being applied in that sector. We must therefore also find practical means of progressively extending them to the informal sector without impairing its capacity to generate employment. (p. 54)

Before undertaking structural adjustment programmes, the industrial organisation in many Latin American countries was characterised by oligopolistic private sector producers and inefficient state monopolies that were overstaffed and subject to bureaucratic excesses. There was a strong argument for economic change to improve the efficiency of the use of resources, but there is a danger that in the process the neo-liberal tide of 'flexibility' may wash away some of the gains in workers' rights that the ILO has campaigned for since its foundation in 1919 (see also Harper and Ramachandran, 1984 and Salomé, 1989).

4.5 *Removing the Bureaucracy: more UIS, more UFS, or more of both?*

Given the economic forces at work in Latin America through de-regulation, privatisation and 'informalisation', what is likely to happen to the balance between the UIS and the UFS in the future? It is easier to consider what will happen in the long run rather than in the short run, as the former is more hypothetical and less likely to collide with inconvenient current facts.

In the long run, if the structural adjustment process does remove distortions and allows markets to operate freely to establish the 'true' relative price of capital to labour, economic theory would predict that the UFS will switch to more labour intensive means of production. Given export-led growth, this would lead to increased UFS employment and sufficient growth could produce a relative (and possibly absolute) fall in the size of the UIS. It would not disappear completely, however, as there would be some who would be unsuitable for work in the UFS and who would need to find niches in the UIS to survive.

In the short run, we are still a long way from long-run neo-classical economic equilibrium and the theory is not well equipped to tell us much about the likely route to that equilibrium. The data presented in Chapter 2 showed that the UIS had grown during the 1980s and the PREALC predictions reported in Section 4.1 suggest that it will continue to grow through the 1990s. This seems plausible in the light of the current processes of 'top-down' and 'bottom-up' informality.

An intriguing question is whether Hernando de Soto's argument is correct: that it is only bureaucracy and an excess of regulations that is preventing those in the UIS from becoming formal. As neo-liberal policies reduce bureaucracy and regulation, what is the evidence that a process of 'formalisation', with UIS enterprises moving into the UFS, is taking place as de Soto predicts?

This is not an easy question to answer, as the hypothesis as stated by de Soto is not sufficiently precise. If the informal entrepreneurs de Soto writes about are rational, they will weigh up the relative *legal* costs and benefits of being 'formal' rather than 'informal' and decide accordingly (see Box 2.1 above).

Rakowski (1994a) takes a pessimistic view of the benefits relative to the legal costs:

A study carried out by Hugo Pirela in 1982 for CORDIPLAN, the Venezuelan National Planning Agency, and research carried out by Liedholm and Mead (1987) in Africa both found that there appears to be a size ceiling on microenterprises growth, efficiency, and profitability, although this varies from place to place depending on the local regulatory context (may be 10, 15, or even 30 workers). Microenterprises must make the leap between that ceiling and significantly larger size in order to compensate for the 'kicking' in of labor legislation, social security, registration costs, payment of taxes, etc. The costs of bridging that gap make it unlikely that microfirms will grow beyond the ceiling. (p. 513)

However, the differences between UIS and UFS enterprises are not only related to questions of legality, but involve other issues, such as the scale of production and the choice of technology. These economic costs and benefits may be more important than the question of legality.

It is clear that UIS enterprises are small in comparison to those in the UFS. This is not merely a matter of the definition chosen but reflects the differences in technology and methods of production. Does becoming 'formal' involve a decision to change size and/or technology, or is it merely a matter of accepting the costs of being legal? If a UIS enterprise paid the legal price and became 'formal', would the benefits it then obtained enable it to compete at its existing size, or would it need to adapt its size and technology to correspond to competing UFS enterprises? If so, what are the implications for increased size and capital?

Villarán (1993, pp. 161–5) presents data on the size distribution of enterprises in Peru in 1987 (see Table 4.4). In this classification, Micro firms correspond to the UIS definition used elsewhere in this book, while Craft firms were 'defined principally in terms of the traditional technology used, with the predominance of manual work, which gives it a high cultural and, in some cases, artistic value' (p. 162). They were usually family firms and although the size range was from one to eight employees, they clearly have many characteristics of UIS enterprises.

What is most striking about the data are the entries in the final column on the average capital/labour ratio (C/L) in US dollars. Making the plausible assumption that these figures represent the amount of capital per worker necessary to operate at a given firm size, then the increments of capital necessary to move up the pyramid to a larger firm size increase very sharply. Legality may give a formerly UIS enterprise greater access to capital, but whether on a scale that would enable it to make the transition is not clear.

The reason it is not clear is that we have very little evidence from

The Future of the Urban Informal Sector

Table 4.4 *Technological Heterogeneity in Peruvian Industry, 1987*

Type of firm	Total EAP Number	(%)	Number of firms	Size Range	No. of jobs	C/L US$
Craft	165000	22.9	55000	1–8	3.0	300
Micro	210670	29.3	84268	1–4	2.5	600
Small	137000	19.0	17125	5–19	8.0	3000
Medium	115230	16.0	2311	20–199	49.9	12000
Large	92000	12.8	206	> 200	446.6	40000
Total	719900	100.0	158910	—	4.5	—

Source: Villarán (1993), p. 163, Table 2.

Key: Size range = number of employees, excluding the employer.

C/L = Average value of the capital used by the enterprise divided by the number of employees in the enterprise and expressed in US$.

research in Latin America on the evolution of enterprises. We do not know what proportion of small firms evolve from being micro-enterprises or, indeed, whether this happens in all but the rarest cases. It is possible that small firms may generally be formed when the entrepreneurs have access to sufficient capital to start operations in the UFS from the outset at the appropriate size.

In the absence of such basic information on the way enterprises deal with different constraints as they evolve, it is not necessarily correct to focus on the legality/illegality dichotomy as being the crucial issue, as de Soto suggests. Much research still needs to be done to resolve this question.

4.6 Conclusions

We have covered a good deal of ground in a relatively short space and the time has come to review the route we followed and to summarise our conclusions.

Chapter 1 pointed out that, unlike Africa or Asia, large-scale rural–urban migration and a decline in the importance of agricultural employment had made many Latin American countries much more like developed countries. The failure of the ISI model of industrialisation to generate enough jobs to absorb the growing urban labour force led many who could not afford to be unemployed to create their own jobs.

Chapter 2 traversed the rocky area of definitional problems and attempted to reconcile different doctrinal approaches to define the UIS. Having argued for a working definition that allowed the UIS to be quantified, the chapter presented statistical data to illustrate what had been happening to the UIS over time, who worked in it and what they did. The links between the UIS and the UFS were explored and the question of whether the UFS exploits the UIS was discussed.

Chapter 3 examined a number of problems facing those working in the UIS. While not all members of the UIS are poor or live in slums or as squatters in self-help housing, there is a considerable overlap between the groups and these were examined. The inadequacy of current social insurance systems in Latin America to protect the poor was evaluated and the possibilities of using subsidies or special targeting was discussed. The particular problems faced by women and children in the UIS was considered.

This final chapter has asked the question of whither the UIS? Clearly this takes us into the realm of speculation. While a number of scenarios may be considered, it is difficult to make any firm predictions about what will happen without assuming that current regional trends and developments will continue.

It seems reasonable to assume that free-market policies, with the removal of regulations, privatisation and a smaller role for the state will spread more widely within Latin America. They are being interpreted as having succeeded in Chile, Argentina and Peru in producing real growth with relatively low rates of inflation and other countries are being urged to follow the same route. Under that assumption, we may note the following possibilities: first, the majority of the countries in Latin America, including the most populous, have high levels of urbanisation (Table 1.1) and many have low fertility rates relative to the region (Table 4.2). This would suggest that future rates of urban growth and of the urban labour force will be lower in these countries. Some of these countries have achieved real economic growth in recent years and this expansion has generated some new UFS employment. However, it is too early to say whether countries such as Argentina, Chile and Peru will be able to sustain this economic growth. In addition, changes in labour market conditions that have been brought about through structural adjustment programmes have produced a degree of 'top-down' informalisation that may act against the creation of UFS jobs. Hence the UIS is likely to continue to play an important role in providing employment for those who are unable to enter the UFS.

Secondly, those countries with relatively low levels of urbanisation, such as Bolivia and the countries of Central America, also tend to have relatively high fertility rates. In some cases, export oriented policies for these countries have stressed agricultural expansion. The form of this expansion has important implications for the labour market. For example, if the agricultural expansion takes the form of capital intensive, large unit production, it could put pressure on agricultural employment. Those who are unable to find work in agriculture may be able to survive through subsistence farming if they have access to land, but many peasants are without formal titles to land and they may be forced to migrate to the cities in search of work. This could lead to an increase in the kind of 'bottom-up' informality that contributed to the growth of the UIS in the countries discussed in the previous paragraph.

One intention of this book has been to help the reader weigh the merits of two views of the UIS. The UIS is extremely heterogeneous and each view concentrates on one aspect. The first view, associated with Hernando de Soto, concentrates on positive aspects of the UIS by stressing the entrepreneurial talent in the sector that is waiting to be released by the neo-liberal policies of deregulation and the reduction of bureaucracy. However, as the data on Peru presented in Chapter 3 show, entrepreneurs represent a very small minority of those working in the UIS, since the majority of UIS workers are self-employed. While some of the self-employed may possess entrepreneurial talent, we have no empirical evidence as to how large the group is.

The second view sees the UIS in a less positive light as being largely the way in which people survive in the cities in the absence of UFS opportunities. From the point of view of numbers, those involved in survival form a majority of those working in the UIS. While there are undoubtedly numbers of microenterprises that generate reasonable incomes and evidence that some choose to work in the UIS, many do not choose to, but are forced to do so by the lack of UFS jobs. In the case of women, the barrier to the UFS is compounded by the problems of segmentation, lack of education and skills as discussed in Chapter 3.

Having surveyed the literature on the UIS in Latin America, Márquez (1994) concludes that:

> The picture of the informal sector that emerges from such studies is of a pyramid. At the top of the pyramid are economically successful informal sector enterprises that employ wage labor and tend to be relatively stable sources of income and employment. At the base are a large number of economic units, many subsistence operations that could not, under any conceivable economic conditions, become stable sources of income and em-

ployment. At the midsection, fluidity is the dominant trait. There are economic units going up from the base pushed by favorable conditions in their particular niche of the market and others coming down from the top crumpled by unfavorable demand and competition. For example, in Venezuela (Márquez and Portela 1991), less than 17 percent of total informal sector employment was generated by enterprises at the top of the pyramid, with the bulk of informal sector employment generated at the base. (p. 166)

This is a picture of survival rather than a sector full of entre-preneurial talent to be celebrated for its potential to create an economic miracle.

From the evidence presented in the text, the author would argue that the second view represents the more realistic picture of life for a majority of those working in the UIS. Within the context of free-market policies, the role of the State is seen as protecting the individual's 'freedom to' undertake profit seeking economic activities and reducing its protection of an individual's 'freedom *from*' hunger, poverty, poor working conditions etc. This change seems unlikely to be reversed in the foreseeable future.

Undoubtedly, the dynamics of the UIS will change over time, but it will continue to be a major component of the urban labour market and the proportion of those working in the UIS who cannot find employment in the UFS, especially women and children, will continue to be important. In other words, 'bottom-up' informality and survival in the city represent crucial characteristics of the UIS and its role in urban development.

Bibliography

Abel, C. and Lewis, C.M. (eds) (1993) *Welfare, Poverty and Development in Latin America* (Basingstoke: Macmillan).

Ahmad, E., Drèze, J., Hills, J. and Sen, A. (eds) (1991) *Social Security in Developing Countries* (Oxford: Clarendon Press).

Angell, A. and Pollack, B. (eds) (1993) *The Legacy of Dictatorship: Political, Economic and Social Change in Pinochet's Chile* (Liverpool: University of Liverpool Institute of Latin American Studies Monograph Series No. 17).

Anker, R. and Hein, C. (eds) (1986) *Sex Inequalities in Urban Employment in the Third World* (Basingstoke: Macmillan).

Annis, S. (1988) 'What is not the same about the urban poor: the case of Mexico City', in Lewis (ed.) (1988), 133–48.

Arturo, R., Avila Avila, O.G. and Avila Avila, R. (1989) 'Poverty and labour market access in Guatemala City', in Rodgers (ed.) (1989), 81–96.

Ashe, J. (1986) *Micro Credit: A Financial Intermediary for the Informal Sector* (Cambridge Mass: ACCION International).

Basok, T. (1993) *Keeping Heads Above Water: Salvadorean Refugees in Costa Rica* (Montreal: McGill-Queen's University Press).

Bechhofer, F. and Elliot, B. (eds) (1981) *The Petite Bourgeoise: Comparative Studies of the Uneasy Stratum* (London: Macmillan).

Beltrán, E. (1988) *Financiamiento de Pequeñas Unidades Productivas* (Lima: Fundación Friedrich Ebert Diagnóstico y Debate No. 29).

Benería, L. (1989) 'Subcontracting and employment dynamics in Mexico City', in Portes, Castells and Benton (eds) (1989), 173–88.

Benería, L. (1992) 'The Mexican debt crisis: restructuring the economy & the household', in Benería and Feldman (eds) (1992), 83–104.

131

Benería, L. and Feldman, S. (eds) (1992) *Unequal Burden: Economic Crises, Persistent Poverty and Women's Work*, (Boulder, CO: Westview Press).

Benton, L. (1986) 'Reshaping the urban core: the politics of housing in authoritarian Uruguay', *Latin American Research Review*, 21 (No. 2), 33–52.

Bequele, A. and Boyden, J. (eds) (1988) *Combating Child Labour* (Geneva: ILO).

Berger, M. and Buvinic, M. (eds) (1988) *La Mujer en al Sector Informal: Trabajo Femenino y Microempresa en América Latina* (Quito: Editorial NUEVA SOCIEDAD).

Berger, M. and Buvinic, M. (eds) (1989) *Women's Ventures: Assistance to the Informal Sector in Latin America* (West Hartford: Kumarian Press).

Birkbeck, C. (1978) 'Self-employed proletarians in an informal factory: the case of Cali's garbage dump', *World Development*, 6 (September/October), 1173–85.

Birkbeck, C. (1979) 'Garbage, industry, and the "vultures" of Cali, Colombia', in Bromley and Gerry (eds) (1979), 161–84.

Blanes Jímenez, J. (1989) 'Cocaine, informality, and the urban economy in La Paz, Bolivia', in Portes, Castells and Benton (eds) (1989), 135–49.

Boltvinik, J. (1994) 'Poverty measurement and alternative indicators', in van der Hoeven and Anker (eds) (1994), 57–83.

Bourque, S.C. and Warren, K.B. (1990) 'Access is not enough: gender perspectives on technology and education', Ch. 6 in Tinker (ed.) (1990), 83–100.

Bowles, W.D. (1988) *A.I.D.'s Experience with Selected Employment Generation Projects* (Washington DC: USAID Evaluation Special Study No. 53).

Boyden, J. (1988) 'National policies and programmes for child workers: Peru', in Bequele and Boyden (eds) (1988), 195–216.

Boyden, J. (1991) 'Working children in Lima, Peru', in Myers (ed.) (1991), 24–45.

Breman, J. (1985) 'A dualist labour system? A critique of the "informal sector" concept', in Bromley (ed.) (1985).

Bridges, J.C. (1980) 'The Mexican family', in Das and Clinton (eds) (1980), 295–334.

Bromley, R. (1978a) 'Introduction – the urban informal sector: why is it worth discussing?', *World Development*, 6 (September/October), 1033–9.

Bromley, R. (1978b) 'Organisation, regulation and exploitation in the so-called "urban informal sector": The street traders of Cali', *World Development*, 6 (September/October), 1161–71.

Bromley, R. (ed.) (1985) *Planning for Small Enterprises in Third World Cities* (Oxford: Pergamon Press).

Bromley, R. (1990) 'A new path to development? The significance and impact of Hernando de Soto's ideas on underdevelopment, production, and reproduction', *Economic Geography*, 66 (October), 328–48.

Bromley, R. (1994) 'Informality, de Soto style: from concept to policy', in Rakowski (ed.) (1994b), 131–51.

Bromley, R. and Gerry, C. (eds) (1979) *Casual Work and Poverty in the Third World* (Chichester: John Wiley).

Brydon, L. and Chant, S. (1989) *Women in the Third World: Gender Issues in Rural and Urban Areas* (Aldershot: Edward Elgar).

Bunster, X. and Chaney, E.M. (1989) *Sellers and Servants: Working Women in Lima, Peru* (Granby: Bergin and Garvey Publishers).

Buvinic, M., Berger, M. and Jaramillo, C. (1989) 'Impact of a credit project for women and men microentrepreneurs in Quito, Ecuador', Ch. 14 in Berger and Buvinic (eds) (1989), 222–46.

Buvinic, M. and Lycette, M.A. (1988) 'Women, poverty and development in the Third World', in Lewis (ed.) (1988), 149–62.

Camazón, D., García-Huidobro, G. and Morgado, H. (1989) 'Labour market performance and urban poverty in Panama', in Rodgers (ed.) (1989), 97–116.

Carbonetto, D. and Carazo M.I. (1986) *Heterogeneidad Tecnológia y Desarrollo Económico: El Sector Informal* (Lima: Fundación Friedrich Ebert).

Carbonetto, D., Hoyle, J. and Tueros, M. (1987) *El Sector Informal Urbano en Lima Metropolitana* (Lima: CEDEP).

Cardoso, E. and Helwege, A. (1992) *Latin America's Economy: Diversity, Trends and Conflicts* (Cambridge MA: MIT Press).

Carlessi, C. (1989) 'The reconquest', NACLA *Report on the Americas*, 23 (November/December), 14–21.

Cartaya, V. (1994) 'Informality and poverty: causal relationship or coincidence?', in Rakowski (ed.) (1994b), 223–49.

Cartier, W.J. and Castañeda, A. (1990) 'Una política de canalización de compras estatales hacia la microempresa: estudio de caso de Manizales, Colombia', in PREALC (1990d), 103–46.

Carvajal, J. (1989) 'Microenterprise as a social investment', in Levitsky (ed.) (1989), 202–7.

Casanovas, R. (1992) 'Informality and illegality, a false identity: the case of Bolivia', in Tokman (ed.) (1992), 23–54.

CEDEFOP (1993) *Vocational Training in Latin America* (Berlin: CEDEFOP).

Chandavarkar, A. (1988) 'The informal sector: empty box or portmanteau concept? (A comment)', *World Development*, 16 (October), 1259–61.

Chant, S. (1985) 'Single-parent families: choice or constraint? The formation of female-headed households in Mexican shanty towns', *Development and Change*, 16 (October), 635–56.

Chant, S. (1991) *Women and Survival in Mexican Cities: Perspectives on Gender, Labour Markets and Low-income Households* (Manchester: University of Manchester Press).

Chant, S. (1992) (ed.) *Gender and Migration in Developing Countries* (London: Belhaven Press).

Christen, R.P. (1989) *What Microenterprise Credit Programs Can Learn from the Moneylenders*, (Cambridge MA: ACCION International Discussion Paper No. 4).

Cole, W.E. and Fayissa, B. (1991) 'The urban subsistence labor force: toward a policy-oriented and empirically accessible taxonomy', *World Development*, 19 (July), 779–89.

Connolly, P. (1985) 'The politics of the informal sector: a critique', in Redclift and Mingione (eds) (1985).

Connolly, P. (1990) 'Dos décadas de "sector informal"', *Sociológia*, 5 (January/April), 75–94.

Contreras, V. and Thomas, J.J. (1993) *Surviving on the Streets: The Ambulatory Street Traders of Santiago* (Santiago: PREALC, World Employment Programme Working Paper No. 375, August).

Contreras, V. and Thomas, J.J. (1994) *The Dynamics of Small Enterprise Evolution in Santiago*, (unpublished manuscript).

Cornia, G.A., Jolly, R. and Stewart, F. (1987) *Adjustment with a Human Face: Volume 1, Protecting the Vulnerable and Promoting Growth* (Oxford: Oxford University Press).

Cornia, G.A. and Stewart, F. (1993) 'Two errors of targeting', *Journal of International Development*, 5 (September/October), 459–96.

Cortes, M., Berry, A. and Ishaq, A. (1987) *Success in Small and Medium-Scale Enterprises: The Evidence from Colombia* (Oxford: Oxford University Press for the World Bank).

Daniels, A. (1986) *Coups and Cocaine: Two Journeys in Latin America* (London: Hutchinson).

Das, M.S. and Clinton, J.J. (eds) (1980) *The Family in Latin America* (New Delhi: Vikas).

de Oliviera, F. (1985) 'A critique of dualist reason: the Brazilian economy since 1930', in Bromley (ed.) (1985).

Desai, M.J. (1979) *Marxian Economics* (Oxford: Basil Blackwell).

Bibliography

Despres, L.A. (1990) 'Macrotheories, microcontexts and the informal sector: case studies of self-employment in three Brazilian cities', in Smith (ed.) (1990), 97–122.

de Soto, H. (1986) *El Otro Sendero: La Revolución Informal* (Lima: Editorial el Barranco).

de Soto, H. (1989a) *The Other Path: The Invisible Revolution in the Third World* (London: I.B. Tauris).

de Soto, H. (1989b) 'Structural adjustment and the informal sector', in Levitsky (ed.) (1989), 3–12.

de Wilde, T., Schreurs, S. and Richman, A. (1991) *Opening the Marketplace to Small Enterprise: Where the Magic Ends and Development Begins* (London: Intermediate Technology Publications).

Dietz, J.L. and Street, J.H. (eds) (1987) *Latin America's Economic Development: Institutionalist and Structuralist Perspectives*, (Boulder CO: Lynne Rienner Publishers).

Drakakis-Smith, D. (ed.) (1986) *Urbanisation in the Developing World* (London: Croom Helm).

Edel, M. and Hellman, R.G. (1989) *Cities in Crisis: The Urban Challenge in the Americas* (New York: Bilden Center for Western Hemisphere Studies).

Elson, D. (ed.) (1991) *Male Bias in the Development Process* (Manchester: University of Manchester Press).

Elson, D. (1992) 'From survival strategies to transformation strategies: women's needs and structural adjustment', in Benería and Feldman (eds) (1992), 26–48.

Fernández-Kelly, M.P. and García, A.M. (1989), 'Informalization at the core: Hispanic women, homework, and the advanced capitalist state', in Portes, Castells and Benton (eds) (1989), 247–64.

Fields, G.S. (1975) 'Rural-urban migration, urban unemployment and underemployment, and job-search activity in LDCs', *Journal of Development Economics*, 2 (June), 165–87.

Fields, G.S. (1990) 'Labour market modelling and the urban informal sector: theory and evidence', in Turnham, Salomé and Schwarz (eds) (1990), 49–69.

Fields, G.S. (1994) 'Poverty changes in developing countries', in van der Hoeven and Anker (eds) (1994), 3–14.

Fields, G.S., Chan, E. and Gindling Jr., T.H. (1985) *The Urban Informal Sector in Malaysia and Costa Rica: Linkages with the Formal Sector* (unpublished manuscript).

Fluitman, F. (ed.) (1989) *Training for Work in the Informal Sector,* (Geneva: ILO).

Folbre, N. (1993) *Women and Social Security in Latin America, the Caribbean and Sub-Saharan Africa* (Geneva: ILO, IDP Women Working Paper No. 5).

FONCODES (1994) *Nota Mensual Numero 5* (Lima: Fondo Nacional de Compensación y Desarrollo Social, June).

Forero Pardo, E. (1991) 'Urban employment and the role of the small-scale manufacturing sector in Colombia', in Thomas, Uribe-Echevarría and Romijn (eds) (1991), 208–30.

Fortuna, J.C. and Prates, S. (1989) 'Informal sector versus informalized labor relations in Uruguay', in Portes, Casells and Benton (eds) (1989), 78–94.

García, A. (1994) 'Identifying and targeting poverty alleviation in Chile', in van der Hoeven and Anker (eds) (1994), 145–49.

García, N.E. (1993) *Ajuste, Reformas y Mercado Laboral: Costa Rica (1980–1990), Chile (1973–1992), México (1981–1991)* (Santiago: PREALC).

Geertz, C. (1963) *Peddlers and Princes: Social Change and Economic Modernization in Two Indonesian Towns* (Chicago: University of Chicago Press).

Gerry, C. and Birkbeck, C. (1981) 'The petty commodity producer in Third World cities: petit-bourgeois or "disguised" proletarian?', in Bechhofer and Elliot (eds) (1981).

Gilbert, A. (1986) 'Self-help housing and state intervention: illustrated reflections on the petty commodity production debate', in Drakakis-Smith (ed.) (1986), 175–91.

Gilbert, A. (1990) *Latin America* (London: Routledge).

Gilbert, A. (1993) 'Self-help housing during recession', in Abel and Lewis (eds) (1993), 109–32.

Gilbert, A. (1994) *The Latin American City* (London: Latin American Bureau).

Gil Díaz, F. (1987) 'Some lessons from Mexico's tax reform', in Newberry and Stern (eds) (1987), 333–59.

Glewwe, P. and de Tray, D. (1989) *The Poor in Latin America During Adjustment: A Case Study of Peru* (Washington DC: World Bank LSMS Working Paper No. 17).

Goodale, G. (1989a) 'Training for women in the informal sector', in Fluitman (ed.) (1989), 47–69.

Goodale, G. (1989b) 'Training for women in the informal sector: the experience of the Pathfinder Fund in Latin America and the Caribbean', in Fluitman (ed.) (1989), 179–88.

Graham, C. (1993) 'From emergency employment to social investment: changing approaches to poverty alleviation in Chile', in Angell and Pollack (eds) (1993), 27–74.

Grosh, M.E. (1990) *Social Spending in Latin America: The Story of the 1980s* (Washington DC: World Bank Discussion Paper No. 106).

Grosh, M.E. (1994) *Administering Targeted Social Programs in Latin America: From Platitudes to Practice* (Washington DC: World Bank).

Grosskoff, R. and Melgar, A. (1990) 'Sector informal urbano: ingreso, empleo y demanda de us producción. El caso uruguayo', in PREALC (1990d), 147–206.

Gugler, J. (ed.) (1988) *The Urbanization of the Third World* (Oxford: Oxford University Press).

Haan, H. (1985) *El Sector Informal en Centroamérica*, (Santiago: PREALC Investigations into Employment No. 27).

Haan, H. (1989a) *Urban Informal Sector Information: Needs and Methods* (Geneva: ILO).

Haan, H. (1989b) 'Two examples of training projects for the informal sector in Central America', in Fluitman (ed.) (1989), 167–71.

Hakim, C. (1992) 'Workforce restructuring, social insurance coverage and the black economy', *Journal of Social Policy*, 18 (June), 471–503.

Hardoy, J.E., Cairncross, S. and Satterthwaite, D. (eds) (1990) *The Poor Die Young: Housing and Health in Third World Cities* (London: Earthscan Publications).

Hardoy, J.E. and Satterthwaite, D. (1989) *Squatter Citizen: Life in the Urban Third World* (London: Earthscan Publications).

Harper, C. (1992) 'La fecundidad y la participación femenina en la fuerza de trabajo', in López, Pollack and Villarreal (eds) (1992), 43–79.

Harper, M. (1989) 'The programme for the development of small enterprises (DESAP) of the Carvajal Foundation in Cali, Colombia', in Fluitman (ed.) (1989), 173–78.

Harper, M. and Ramachandran, K. (1984) *Small Business Promotion: Case Studies from Developing Countries* (London: Intermediate Technology Publications).

Harris, J.R. and Todaro, M.P. (1970) 'Migration, unemployment and development: a two-sector analysis', *American Economic Review*, 60 (March), 126–42.

Harriss, J.C. (1990) *Linkages Between the Formal and the Informal Sectors in Developing Countries: A Review of Literature* (Geneva:

ILO World Employment Programme Working Paper, WEP 2–19/WP.50).

Harriss, J.C. and Moore, M. (eds) (1984) *Development and the Rural-Urban Divide* (London: Frank Cass).

Hart, K. (1973) 'Informal income opportunities and urban employment in Ghana', *Journal of Modern African Studies*, 11, 61–89.

Hellman, J.A. (1986) 'Migration and urbanisation: breaking new ground', *Latin American Research Review*, 21 (No. 3), 216–26.

Herrick, B. and Hudson, B. (1981) *Urban Poverty and Economic Development: A Case Study of Costa Rica* (London: Macmillan).

Hirata, H. and Humphrey, J. (1991) 'Workers' response to job loss: female and male industrial workers in Brazil', *World Development*, 19 (June), 671–82.

Horton, S., Kanbur, R. and Mazumdar, D. (eds) (1994a) *Labor Markets in an Era of Adjustment, Volume 1: Issue Papers* (Washington DC: World Bank Economic Development Institute).

Horton, S., Kanbur, R. and Mazumdar, D. (eds) (1994b) *Labor Markets in an Era of Adjustment, Volume 2: Case Studies* (Washington DC: World Bank Economic Development Institute).

IDB (1990) *Economic and Social Progess in Latin America: 1990 Report* (Washington DC: Inter-American Development Bank).

IDESI (1991a) *El Empleo y El Sector Informal en Arequipa Metropolitana* (Lima: Instituto de Desarrollo del Sector Informal).

IDESI (1991b) *El Empleo y El Sector Informal en Cuzco Metropolitano* (Lima: Instituto de Desarrollo del Sector Informal).

IDESI (1991c) *El Empleo y El Sector Informal en Ica Metropolitana* (Lima: Instituto de Desarrollo del Sector Informal).

IDESI (1991d) *El Empleo y El Sector Informal en Iquitos Metropolitano* (Lima: Instituto de Desarrollo del Sector Informal).

IDESI (1991e) *El Empleo y El Sector Informal en Puno y Juliaca Metropolitana* (Lima: Instituto de Desarrollo del Sector Informal).

IDESI (1991f) *El Empleo y El Sector Informal en Trujillo Metropolitano* (Lima: Instituto de Desarrollo del Sector Informal).

ILO (1972) *Employment, Incomes and Equality: A Strategy for Increasing Productive Employment in Kenya* (Geneva: ILO).

ILO (1988) *Assessing the Impact of Statutory Minimum Wages in Developing Countries: Four Case Studies* (Geneva: ILO, Labour–Management Relations Series No. 67).

ILO (1991a) *The Dilemma of the Informal Sector* (Geneva: ILO Report of the Director-General, International Labour Conference, 78th Session).

ILO (1991b) *The Urban Informal Sector in Africa in Retrospect and Prospect: An Annotated Bibliography* (Geneva: ILO).

ILO (1992) *The Urban Informal Sector in Asia: An Annotated Bibliography* (Geneva: ILO).

INEGI (1990) *Medición del Sector Informal en Mexico* (Aguascalientes, Mexico: Instituto de Estadística Geografía e Informática).

Infante, R. (ed.) (1993) *Social Debt: The Challenge of Equity* (Santiago: PREALC).

Jatobá, J. (1989) 'Urban poverty, labour markets and regional differentiation in Brazil', in Rodgers (ed.) (1989), 35–64.

Khan, A.R. (1993) *Structural Adjustment and Income Distribution: Issues and Experience* (Geneva: ILO World Employment Programme).

Khundker, N. (1988) 'The fuzziness of the informal sector: can we afford to throw out the baby with the bath water? (A comment)', *World Development*, 16 (October), 1263–5.

King, K. (1974) 'Kenya's informal machine makers: a study of small-scale industry in Kenya's emergent artisan society', *World Development*, 2 (April/May), 9–28.

King, K. (1989) 'Training for the urban informal sector in developing countries: policy issues for practitioners', Chap. 2 in Fluitman (ed.) (1989), 17–38.

Klein, E. and Tokman, V.E. (1993) *Informal Sector and Regulations in Ecuador and Jamaica* (Paris: OECD Development Centre Technical Paper No. 86, August).

Kleinekathoefer, M. (1987) *El Sector Informal Integración o Transformación: Consideraciones en Torno a una Nueva Política de Formento* (Santo Domingo: Fundación Friedrich Ebert).

Lagos, R.A. (1992) 'Barriers to legality and their costs for the informal sector', in Tokman (ed.) (1992), 87–107.

Lanzetta de Pardo, M., Murillo Cansaño, G. and Triana Soto, A. (1989) 'The articulation of formal and informal sectors in the economy of Bogotá, Colombia', in Portes, Castells and Benton (eds) (1989), 95–110.

Levitsky, J. (ed.) (1989) *Microenterprises in Developing Countries* (London: Intermediate Technology Publications).

Lewin, A.C. (1985) 'The dialectic of dominance: petty production and peripheral capitalism', in Bromley (ed.) (1985).

Lewis, J.P. (ed.) (1988) *Strengthening the Poor: What Have We Learned?* (Washington DC: Overseas Development Council).

Lewis, O. (1958) *Five Families* (New York: Random House).

Lewis, O. (1969) *La Vida: Studies in the Culture of Poverty in San Juan and New York* (New York: Random House).

Lewis, W.A. (1954) 'Economic development with unlimited supplies of labour', *Manchester School*, 22, 139–91.

Liedholm, C. and Mead, D. (1987) *Small Scale Industries in Developing Countries: Empirical Evidence and Policy Implications* (East Lancing: Michigan State University International Development Paper No. 9).

Lloyd, P. (1980) *The 'Young Towns' of Lima: Aspects of Urbanization in Peru* (Cambridge: Cambridge University Press).

Lloyd, P. (1982) *A Third World Proletariat?* (London: George Allen and Unwin).

Lloyd-Sherlock, P. (1992) *Social Insurance Reform in an Ageing World: The Case of Latin America* (London: London School of Economics, STICERD Development Economics Research Programme Working Paper No. 39, August).

Lomnitz, L. (1988) 'The social and economic organization of a Mexican shanty town', in Gugler (ed.) (1988), 242–63.

López, C., Pollack, M. and Villarreal, M. (eds) (1992) *Genero y Mercado de Trabajo en América Latina* (Santiago: PREALC).

Lubell, H. (1991) *The Informal Sector in the 1980s and 1990s*, (Paris: OECD Development Centre).

Lycette, M. and White, K. (1989) 'Improving women's access to credit in Latin America and the Caribbean: policy and project recommendations', in Berger and Buvinic (eds) (1989), 19–44.

Machado, L.M.V. (1987) 'The problems for woman-headed households in a low-income housing programme in Brazil', in Moser and Peake (eds) (1987), 55–69.

Mangin, W.P. (1967) 'Latin American squatter settlements: a problem and a solution', *Latin American Research Review*, 2 (No. 3), 65–98.

Mangin, W.P. (ed.) (1970) *Peasants in Cities: Readings in the Anthropology of Urbanization* (Boston: Houghton Mifflin).

Márquez, G. (1994) 'Inside informal sector policies in Latin America: an economist's view', in Rakowski (ed.) (1994b), 153–73.

Márquez, G. and Portela, C. (1991) 'Los informales urbanos en Venezuela: ¿Pobres o eficientes?', in Márquez and Portela (eds) (1991), 1–41.

Márquez, G. and Portela, C. (eds) (1991) *La Economía Informal* (Caracas: IESA).

Mazumdar, D. (1975) *The Theory of Urban Unemployment in Less Developed Countries* (Washington DC: World Bank Staff Working Paper No. 198).

Mazumdar, D. (1976a) 'The urban informal sector', *World Development*, 4 (August), 655–79.

Mazumdar, D. (1976b) 'The rural–urban wage gap, migration and the shadow wage', *Oxford Economic Papers*, 28, 406–25.

McFarren, W. (1992) 'The politics of Bolivia's economic crisis: survival strategies of displaced tin-mining households', in Tinker (ed.) (1990), 131–58.

McGee, T.G. (1973) 'Peasants in the cities: a paradox, a paradox, a most ingenious paradox', *Human Organization*, 25 (No. 1), 128–40.

McKean, C.S. (1994) 'Training and technical assistance for small and microenterprises: a discussion of their effectiveness', in Rakowski (ed.) (1994b), 199–219.

McKee, K. (1988) 'Micro level strategies for supporting livelihood, employment and income generating of poor women in the Third World: the challenge of significance', paper submitted to the Ford Foundation symposium on *Expanding Income Earning Opportunities for Women in Poverty: A Cross Regional Dialogue* (Kenya: Nairobi, May).

Mesa-Lago, C. (1991) 'Social security in Latin America and the Caribbean: a comparative assessment', in Ahmad, Drèze, Hills and Sen (eds) (1991), 356–94.

Mesa-Lago, C. (1992) 'Protection for the informal sector in Latin America and the Caribbean by social security or alternative means', in Tokman (ed.) (1992), 169–206.

Mesa-Lago, C. (1994) *Changing Social Security in Latin America: Towards Alleviating the Social Costs of Economic Reform* (Boulder CO: Lynne Rienner).

Mezzera, J. (1987) *Crédito y Capacitación para el Sector Informal* (Santiago: PREALC).

Mezzera, J. (1989) 'Excess labor supply and the urban informal sector: an analytical framework', in Berger and Buvinic (1989).

Mezzera, J. (ed.) (1993) *Crédito Informal: Acceso al Sistema Financiero* (Santagio: PREALC).

Middleton, A. (1991) *La Dinamica del Sector Informal Urbano en el Ecuador* (Quito: CIRE).

MIDEPLAN (1992) *Población, Educación, Vivienda, Salud, Empleo y Pobreza: CASEN 1990* (Santiago: Ministry of Planning and Co-operation).

Mohan, R. (1986) *Work, Wages, and Welfare in a Developing Metropolis: Consequences of Growth in Bogotá, Colombia* (Oxford: Oxfxord University Press for the World Bank).

Morrison, A.R. and May, R.A. (1994) 'Escape from terror: violence and migration in post-revolutionary Guatemala', *Latin American Research Review*, 29 (No. 2), 111–32.

Moser, C.O.N. (1978) 'Informal sector or petty commodity production: dualism or dependence in urban development', *World Development*, 6 (September/October), 1041–64.

Moser, C.O.N. (1984) 'The informal sector reworked: viability and vulnerability in urban development', *Regional Development Dialogue*, 5, 135–78.

Moser, C.O.N. and Peake, L. (eds) (1987) *Women, Human Settlements and Housing* (London: Tavistock Publications).

Murphy, A.D. and Rees, M.W. (1990) 'Crisis and sector in Oaxaca, Mexico: a comparison of households 1977–1987', in Smith (ed.) (1990), 1147–59.

Murphy, M.F. (1990) 'The need for a re-evaluation of the concept "informal sector": the Dominican case', in Smith (ed.) (1990), 161–81.

Myers, W.E. (ed.) (1991) *Protecting Working Children* (London: Zed Books and UNICEF).

Nash, J. and Safa, H. (eds) (1985) *Women and Change in Latin America* (New York: Bergin and Garvey).

Newberry, D. and Stern, N.H. (eds) (1987) *Modern Tax Theory for Developing Countries* (Oxford: Oxford University Press).

Nientied, P. and van der Linden, J. (1988) 'Approaches to low-income housing in the Third World', in Gugler (ed.) (1988), 138–56.

Norris, W.P. (1990) 'Informal sector housing: social structure and the state in Brazil', in Smith (ed.) (1990), 73–96.

Nuss, S. (1989) *Women in the World of Work: Statistical Analysis and Projections to the Year 2000* (Geneva: ILO).

Otero, M. (1989a) *A Question of Impact: Solidarity Group Programs and Their Approach to Evaluation* (Tegucigalpa: ASEPADE).

Otero, M. (1989b) 'Benefits, costs and sustainability of microenterprise assistance programmes', in Levitsky (ed.) (1989), 211–23.

Otero, M. (1994) 'The role of governments and private institutions in addressing the informal sector in Latin America', in Rakowski (ed.) (1994b), 177–97.

Peattie, L. (1987) 'An idea in good currency and how it grew: the informal sector', *World Development*, 15 (July), 851–60.

Pérez-Alemán, P. (1992) 'Economic crisis & women in Nicaragua', Chap. 10 in Tinker (ed.) (1990), 239–58.

Pérez Sáinz, J.P. (1991) *Informalidad Urbana en América Latina: Enfoques, Problemáticas e Interrogantes* (Caracas: Editorial Nueva Sociedad).

Pérez Sáinz, J.P. and Menjívar Larín, R. (eds) (1991) *Informalidad Urbana en Centroamérica: Entre la Acumulación y la Subsistencia* (San José, Costa Rica: FLACSO).

Pérez Sáinz, J.P. and Menjívar Larín, R. (1994) 'Central American men and women in the urban informal sector', *Journal of Latin American Studies*, 26 (May), 431–47.

Perlman, J.E. (1976) *The Myth of Marginality: Urban Poverty and Politics in Rio de Janeiro* (Berkeley: University of California Press).

Pinilla, S. (1986) *Concepción, Características y Promoción del Sector Informal Urbano* (Lima: Instituto de Desarrollo del Sector Informal).

Placencia, M.M. (1989) 'Training and credit programs for microentrepreneurs: some concerns about the training of women', in Berger and Buvinic (eds) (1989), 121–31.

Plant, G. (1994) *Labour Standards and Structural Adjustment* (Geneva: ILO).

Pollack, M. (1989) 'Poverty and the labour market in Costa Rica', in Rodgers (ed.) (1989), 65–80.

Pollack, M. and Uthoff, A. (1989) 'Poverty and the labour market: Greater Santiago, 1969–85', in Rodgers (ed.) (1989), 117–43.

Portes, A. (1989) 'Latin American urbanization during the years of the crisis, *Latin American Research Review*, 24 (No. 3), 7–44.

Portes, A., Blitzer, S. and Curtis, J. (1986) 'The urban informal sector in Uruguay: its internal structure, characteristics and effects', *World Development*, 15 (June), 727–41.

Portes, A., Castells, M. and Benton, L.A. (1989) *The Informal Economy: Studies in Advanced and Less Developed Countries* (Baltimore: Johns Hopkins University Press).

PREALC (1982) *Mercado de Trabajo en Cifras: 1950–1980* (Santiago: PREALC).

PREALC (1986) *La Evolución del Empleo Formal e Informal en el Sector Servicios Latinamericano* (Santiago: PREALC, World Employment Programme Working Paper No. 279, September).

PREALC (1987a) *Notes on Segmented Labour Markets in Urban Areas* (Santiago: PREALC, World Employment Programme Working Paper No. 289, February).

PREALC (1987b) *La Microempresa en la Rama de la Confección: Estudios de Casos en la Ciudad de Lima* (Santiago: PREALC, World Employment Programme Working Paper No. 295, April).

PREALC (1987c) *Pobresa y Mercado de Trabajo en el Gran Santiago, 1969–1985* (Santiago: PREALC, World Employment Programme Working Paper No. 299, June).

PREALC (1987d) *Ciclo Económico, Mercado de Trabajo y Pobresa: Gran Santiago, 1969–1985* (Santiago: PREALC, World Employment Programme Working Paper No. 303, July).

PREALC (1987e) *Las Migraciones a Lima Metropolitana, Crisis Económica y Cambios en la Inserción de los Migrantes* (Santiago: PREALC, World Employment Programme Working Paper No. 304, August).

PREALC (1988) *Sobrevivir en la Calle: El Comercio Ambulante en Santiago* (Santiago: PREALC).

PREALC (1990a) *Lecciones sobre Crédito al Sector Informal* (Santiago: PREALC).

PREALC (1990b) *Mas Alla de la Regulación: El Sector Informal en América Latina* (Santiago: PREALC).

PREALC (1990c) *Urbanización y Sector Informal en America Latina, 1960–1980* (Santiago: PREALC).

PREALC (1990d) *Ventas Informales: Relaciones con el Sector Moderno* (Santiago: PREALC).

PREALC (1990e) *Employment and Equity: The Challenge of the 1990s* (Santiago: PREALC, World Employment Programme Working Paper No. 354, October).

PREALC (1991a) *Labour Market Adjustment in Latin America: An Appraisal of the Social Effects in the 1980s* (Santiago: PREALC, World Employment Programme Working Paper No. 357, May).

PREALC (1991b) *Retrospectiva del Sector Informal Urbano en América Latina: una Bibliografía Anotada* (Santiago: PREALC).

PREALC (1993), 'Latin America: economic growth that generates more jobs, of inferior quality', *Newsletter* (No. 32, September)

Priestley, G. (1989) 'Squatters, oligarchs and soldiers in San Miguelito, Panama', in Edel and Hellman (eds) (1989), 127–56.

Pryer, J. and Crook, N. (1988) *Cities of Hunger: Urban Malnutrition in Developing Countries* (Oxford: OXFAM Publications).

Radcliffe, S.A. (1992) 'Mountains, maidens and migration: gender and mobility in Peru', in Chant (ed.) (1992), 30–48.

Rakowski, C.A. (1994a) 'Convergence and divergence in the informal sector debate: a focus on Latin America, 1984–92', *World Development*, 22 (April), 501–16.

Rakowski, C.A. (1994b) *Contrapunto: The Informal Sector Debate in Latin America* (Albany: State University of New York Press).

Ramírez, J. (1989) 'Training for informal sector enterprises in Latin America', in Fluitman (ed.) (1989), 159–66.

Redclift, N. and Mingione, E. (eds) (1985) *Beyond Employment: Household, Gender and Subsistence* (Oxford: Basil Blackwell).

Reichmann, R. (1989) 'Women's participation in two PVO credit programs for microenterprise: cases from the Dominican Republic and Peru', in Berger and Buvinic (eds) (1989), 132–60.

Reichmuth, M. (1978) *Dualism in Peru: an investigation into the interrelationships between Lima's informal clothing industry and the formal sector* (Oxford, BLitt thesis, unpublished).

Remenyi, J. (1991) *Where Credit is Due: Income-Generating Programmes for the Poor in Developing Countries* (London: Intermediate Technology Publications).

Reynolds, L.G. (1969) 'Economic development with surplus labour: some complications', *Oxford Economic Papers*, 21, 89–103.

Ribe, H., Carvalho, S., Liebenthal, R., Nicholas, P. and Zuckerman, E. (1990) *How Structural Adjustment Programs Can Help the Poor: The World Bank's Experience* (Washington DC: World Bank Discussion Paper No. 17).

Roberts, B. (1989) 'Employment structure, life cycle, and life chances: formal and informal sectors in Guadalajara', in Portes, Castells and Benton (eds) (1989), 41–60.

Roberts, B. (1990) 'The informal sector in comparative perspective', in M.E. Smith (ed.) (1990).

Rodgers, G. (ed.) (1989) *Urban Poverty and the Labour Market: Access to Jobs and Incomes in Asian and Latin American Cities* (Geneva: ILO).

Rondinelli, D. and Cheema, G.S. (eds) (1988) *Urban Services in Developing Countries: Public and Private Roles in Urban Development* (Basingstoke: Macmillan).

Rossini, R. and Thomas, J.J. (1990) 'The size of the informal sector in Peru: a critical comment on Hernando de Soto's *El Otro Sendero*', *World Development*, 18 (January), 125–35.

Sachs, J.D. (ed.) (1989) *Developing Country Debt and the World Economy* (Chicago: University of Chicago Press for the National Bureau of Economic Research).

Safa, H.I. (1987) 'Urbanization, the informal economy and state policy in Latin America', in Smith and Feagin (eds) (1987), 252–72.

Salazar, M.C. (1988) 'Child labour in Colombia: Bogotá's quarries and brickyards', in Bequele and Boyden (eds) (1988), 49–60.

Salmen, L.F. (1987) *Listen to the People: Participant-observer Evaluation of Development Projects* (Oxford: Oxford University Press for the World Bank).

Salomé, B. (ed.) (1989) *Fighting Urban Unemployment in Developing Countries* (Paris: OECD Development Centre).

Sánchez, C.E., Palmiero, H. and Farrero, F. (1981) 'The informal and quasi-formal sectors in Córdoba', in Sethuraman (ed.) (1981), 144–58.

Santos, M. (1979) *The Shared Space – The Two Circuits of Urban Economy and their Spatial Recercussions* (London: Methuen).

Sanyal, B. (1988) 'The urban informal sector revisited: some notes on the relevance of the concept in the 1980s', *Third World Planning Review*, 10 (February), 65–83.

Schaefer, K. (assisted by C.R. Spindel) (1976) *São Paulo: Urban Development and Employment* (Geneva: ILO).

Scheper-Hughes, N. and Hoffman, D. (1994) 'Kids out of place', *NACLA Report on the Americas*, 27 (May/June), 16–23.

Schmitz, H. (1982) *Manufacturing in the Backyard: Case Studies on Accumulation and Employment in Small-scale Brazilian Industry* (London: Frances Pinter).

Scott, A. MacEwan (1979) 'Who are the self-employed?', in Bromley and Gerry (eds) (1979).

Scott, A. MacEwan (1982) 'Changes in the structure of child labour under conditions of dualistic economic growth', *Development and Change*, 13 (October), 537–50.

Scott, A. MacEwan (1986) 'Economic development and urban women's work: the case of Lima, Peru', in Anker and Hein (eds) (1986), 313–69.

Scott, A. MacEwan (1991) 'Informal sector or female sector?: gender bias in urban labour market models', in Elson (ed.) (1991).

Scott, A. MacEwen (1994) *Divisions and Solidarities: Gender, Class and Employment in Latin America* (London: Routledge).

Selby, H.A., Murphy, A.D. and Lorenzen, S.A. (1990) *The Mexican Urban Household: Organizing for Self-Defense* (Austin: University of Texas Press).

Sen, A.K. (1983) 'Poor, relatively speaking', *Oxford Economic Papers*, 35 (March), 153–69.

Sen, A.K. (1984) *Resources, Values and Development* (Oxford: Basil Blackwell).

Sethuraman, S.V. (1976) 'The urban informal sector: concept, measurement and policy', *International Labour Review*, 114 (July/August), 69–81.

Sethuraman, S.V. (ed.) (1981) *The Urban Informal Sector in Developing Countries: Employment, Poverty and Environment* (Geneva: ILO).

Singer, H. (1992) *Research of the World Employment Programme: Future Priorities and Selective Assessment* (Geneva: ILO).

Smith, M.E. (ed.) (1990) *Perspectives on the Informal Economy* (London: University Press of America).

Smith, M.P. and Feagin, J.R. (eds) (1987) *The Capitalist City: Global Restructuring and Community Politics* (Oxford: Basil Blackwell).

Souza, P.R. and Tokman, V.E. (1976) 'The informal urban sector in Latin America', *International Labour Review*, 114 (November/December), 355–65.

Späth, B. (ed.) (1993) *Small Firms and Development in Latin America: The Role of the Institutional Environment, Human Resources and Industrial Relations* (Geneva: International Institute for Labour Studies).

Standing, G. and Tokman, V. (eds) (1991) *Towards Social Adjustment: Labour Market Issues in Structural Adjustment* (Geneva: ILO).

Stearns, K. (1991) *The Hidden Beast: Delinquency in Microenterprise Credit Programs* (Cambridge MA: ACCION International Discussion Papers No. 5).

Stearns, K. and Otero, M. (eds) (1990) *The Critical Connection: Governments, Private Institutions, and the Informal Sector in Latin America* (Cambridge MA: ACCION International Monograph Series No. 5).

Strassmann, W.P. (1986) 'Types of neighbourhood and home-based enterprises: evidence from Lima, Peru', *Urban Studies*, 23 (December), 485–500.

Streeten, P. (1994) 'Poverty concepts and measurement', in van der Hoeven and Anker (eds) (1994), 15–30.

Thomas, H., Uribe-Echevarría, F. and Romijn, H. (eds) (1991) *Small-scale Production: Strategies for Industrial Restructuring* (London: Intermediate Technology Publications).

Thomas, J.J. (1990/91) 'Peru and the informal economy', *Third World Quarterly*, 12 (Nos. 3/4), 167–72.

Thomas, J.J. (1992a) *Informal Economic Activity* (Hemel Hempstead: Harvester Wheatsheaf).

Thomas, J.J. (1992b) 'Whatever happened to the urban informal sector? The regressive effect of "Double Dualism" on the financial analysis of developing countries', *Bulletin of Latin American Research*, 11 (September), 279–94.

Thomas, J.J. (1993a) *The Links Between Structural Adjustment and Poverty: Causal or Remedial?* (Santiago: PREALC WEP Working Paper No. 373, January).

Thomas, J.J. (1993b) *Replicating the Grameen Bank: the Latin American Experience* (London: London School of Economics, mimeograph, April).

Thomas, J.J. (1993c) *On the Use of 'Control' Groups in the Evaluation of Credit Programmes* (London: London School of Economics, mimeograph, April).

Thorp, R. (1990) Book review of de Soto's *The Other Path*, *Journal of Latin American Studies*, 22 (Part 2), 403–5.

Tinker, I. (ed.) (1990) *Persistent Inequalities: Women and World Development* (Oxford: Oxford University Press).

Tokman, V.E. (1978a) 'An exploration into the nature of informal/formal sector relationships', *World Development*, 6 (September/October), 1065–76.

Tokman, V.E. (1978b) 'Competition between the informal and formal sectors in retailing: the case of Santiago', *World Development*, 6 (September/October), 1187–98.

Tokman, V.E. (1987) 'Unequal development and the absorption of labor', in Dietz and Street (eds) (1987), 228–40.

Tokman, V.E. (1989) 'Policies for a heterogeneous informal sector in Latin America', *World Development*, 17 (July), 1067–76.

Tokman, V.E. (1990) 'The informal sector in Latin America: fifteen years later', in Turnham, Salomé and Schwarz (eds) (1990), 94–109.

Tokman, V.E. (1991) 'The informal sector in Latin America: from underground to legality', in Standing and Tokman (eds) (1991), 141–57.

Tokman, V.E. (ed.) (1992) *Beyond Regulation: The Informal Economy in Latin America* (Santiago: PREALC).

Tosta Berkinck, M., Bovo, J.M. and Cintra, L.C. (1981) 'The urban informal sector and industrial development in a small city: the case of Caminas', in Sethuraman (ed.) (1981), 159–67.

Turner, J.F.C. (1967) 'Barriers and channels for housing development in modernizing countries', *Journal of the American Institute of Planners*, 33 (No. 2), 167–81.

Turner, J.F.C. (1968) 'Housing priorities, settlement patterns and urban development in modernizing countries', *Journal of the American Institute of Planners*, 34 (No. 4), 354–63.

Turnham, D. (1993) *Employment and Development: A New Review of Evidence* (Paris: OECD Development Centre).

Turnham, D., Salomé, B. and Schwarz, A. (eds) (1990) *The Informal Sector Revisited* (Paris: OECD Development Centre).

UN (1989) *1989 World Survey on the Role of Women in Development* (Washington DC: UN).

UNDP (1993) *Human Development Report 1993* (Oxford: Oxford University Press for the United Nations Development Programme).

USAID (1985a) *The PISCES II Experience: Local Efforts in Microenterprise Development* (Washington DC: US Agency for International Development).

USAID (1985b) *The PISCES II Experience: Case Studies from Dominican Republic, Costa Rica, Kenya and Egypt* (Washington DC: US Agency for International Development).

Uzzell, J.D. (1980) 'Mixed strategies and the informal sector: three faces of reserve labor', *Human Organization*, 39 (Spring), 40–9.

van der Hoeven, R. and Anker, R. (eds) (1994) *Poverty Monitoring: An International Concern* (Basingstoke: Macmillan).

van der Linden, J. (1986) *The Sites and Services Approach Reviewed* (Aldershot: Gower).

van Lindert, P. and Verkoren, O. (1994) *Bolivia: A Guide to the People, Politics and Culture* (London: Latin America Bureau).

Velenchik, A.D. (1993) *Apprenticeship Contracts and Credit Markets in Ghana*, (unpublished manuscript).

Villarán, F. (1993) 'Small-scale industry efficiency groups in Peru', in Späth (ed.) (1993), 158–95.

Vittas, D. and Iglesias, A. (1992) *The Rationale and Performance of Personal Pension Plans in Chile* (Washington DC: World Bank Working Paper No. 867).

Walton, J. (1987) 'Urban protest and the global political economy: the IMF riots', in Smith and Feagin (eds.) (1987), 364–86.

Ward, P. (ed.) (1982) *Self-Help Housing: A Critique* (London: Mansell).

Williams, G. and Mutebile, T. (1978) 'Petty commodity production in Nigeria: a note', *World Development*, 6 (September/October), 1103–4.

World Bank (1986) *World Development Report 1986* (Oxford: Oxford University Press for the World Bank).

World Bank (1988) *World Development Report 1988* (Oxford: Oxford University Press for the World Bank).

World Bank (1989a) *World Tables, 1988–89* (Baltimore: Johns Hopkins University Press for the World Bank).

World Bank (1989b) *Peru: Policies to Stop Hyperinflation and Initiate Economic Recovery* (Washington DC: World Bank).

World Bank (1990a) *World Development Report 1990* (Oxford: Oxford University Press for the World Bank).

World Bank (1990b) *Making Adjustment Work for the Poor: A Framework for Policy Reform in Africa* (Washington DC: World Bank).

World Bank (1990c) *The Social Dimensions of Adjustment in Africa: A Policy Agenda* (Washington DC: World Bank).

World Bank (1993a) *World Development Report 1993* (Oxford: Oxford University Press for the World Bank).

World Bank (1993b) *Peru: Poverty Assessment and Social Policies and Programs for the Poor* (Washington DC: World Bank Report No. 111910–PE, May).

World Bank (1993c) *Latin America and the Caribbean: A Decade after the Debt Crisis* (Washington DC: World Bank Latin America and the Caribbean Regional Office).

World Bank (1994a) *World Development Report 1994* (Oxford: Oxford University Press for the World Bank).

World Bank (1994b) *World Tables, 1994* (Baltimore: Johns Hopkins University Press for the World Bank).

Wurgaft, J. (1993) *Fondos de Inversión Social en América Latina* (Santiago: PREALC).

Yunus, M. (1989) 'Grameen Bank: organization and operation', in Levitsky (ed.) (1989), 144–61.

Author Index

151

Author Index

Subject Index

'self–help' housing 96
SENA 113
'site-and-services' programmes 100
slums 96
   clearances 99
small enterprises 40
social insurance 89–93
   'Bismarkian model' of 89
   statutory versus statistical
     coverage 90
social protection 93–6
   extending to UIS 93
squatter settlements 96
street children 87–9
street traders 67, 76
structural adjustment programme
   (SAP) 7
sub-contracting 58–9, 107–8,
   123–4
subsidies 93–6
   effectiveness versus efficiency
     94–6
   versus targeting 94–6
supply-side support for the UIS
   112–20
survival in the city 130

targeting 94–6
   characteristic screening 94
   effectiveness versus efficiency
     94–6
   locational screening 95
   versus subsidies 94–6
'top-down' informality 123, 125,
   129
Total External Debt 7
Total Fertility Rate (TFR) 108
training programmes 112–4,
   116–8

training programmes *continued*
   and credit programmes 116–8
   constraints on women in 117
   for microenterprises 114
'trickle down' 7
Trujillo 52–5

UNDP 107
urban-rural bias 93
urban formal sector
   capital/labour ratio in 127
   poverty in 72–3
urban informal sector 10–12
   capital/labour ratio in 127
   children in 85–9
   demand-side support for 120–4
   falling earnings during debt
     crisis 121
   housing and 96–102
   income distribution in 51
   place of work 50
   positive discrimination towards
     122
   poverty and the UIS 70–3
   productivity of 42
   size of 39–47
   supply-side support for 112–20
urbanisation 1, 96–8
Uruguay 1, 68, 99

Venezuela 68, 72
vocational skills 77

World Bank
   reaction to UNICEF criticisms
     94
World Employment Programme
   (WEP) 18

Pluto Latin American Studies

Theorizing Social Movements

Joe Foweraker

In this first title of a major new series on Latin American politics, Joe Foweraker presents and clarifies the main theories of social movements and provides a critical account of their application in Latin America.

The work is in four parts: theories of social movements; class analysis and social movement theory; social movements related to their political environment and institutional links; and the fate of social movements under the newly liberal and democratic regimes in Latin America.

ISBN hardback 0 7453 0713 2; softback 0 7453 0714 0

Also published by Pluto Press

Barbaric Others

ZIA SARDAR, ASHIS NANDY & MERRYL WYN DAVIES

This is a unique perspective on an adversarial world-view that has allowed the West to see other peoples as barbarians, infidels, even 'savages'. In exposing this convenient myopia, the authors provide a succinct and shameful history of the racism and xenophobia that have shaped western thought from ancient Greece to the present day.

ISBNs hardback: 0 7453 0742 6; softback: 0 7453 0743 4

Order from your local bookseller or contact the publisher on 0181 348 2724.

Pluto Press

345 Archway Road, London N6 5AA
140 Commerce Street, East Haven, CT 06512, USA

Published by Pluto Press

TEARS OF THE CROCODILE

From Rio to Reality in the Developing World

Neil Middleton, Phil O'Keefe with Sam Mayo

❏ The first significant reassessment of the goals and objectives of the Rio summit

The industrialised world has turned its big guns on the poor. Threatened by a vast recession and a tottering financial system and struggling to extricate itself from the post-Cold War wreckage, it has put all its energies into self-defence by constructing fiercely protectionist trade blocs. Nowhere has this been more publicly apparent than at the much trumpeted UN 'Earth Summit', held in Rio de Janeiro in 1992.

Tears of the Crocodile examines what exactly happened in Rio, focusing specifically on the complex issues that perpetuate inequity, poverty and hunger. The authors offer a powerful argument that the Rio environmental agenda was about preserving Northern interests, and that these critical issues were not addressed.

ISBN hardback: 0 7453 0764 7   softback: 0 7453 0765 5

Order from your local bookseller or contact the publisher on 0181 348 2724.

Pluto Press
345 Archway Road, London N6 5AA
140 Commerce Street, East Haven, CT06512, USA